IMAGES
of America

GERMANTOWN, MOUNT AIRY, AND CHESTNUT HILL

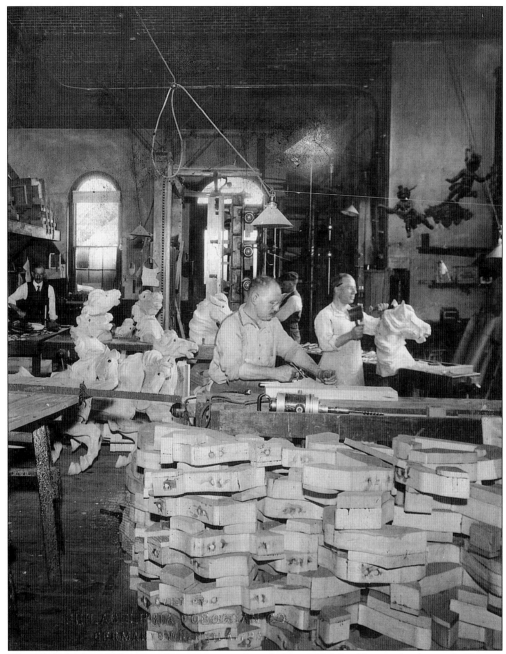

The Philadelphia Toboggan Company was founded in 1904 by Henry Auchy and Chester Albright. Famous for its carousels, which were sold around the world, it is also the oldest roller coaster manufacturer in the world ("toboggans" are roller coaster cars). Eighty-seven carousels were built in the PTC factory at 130 East Duval Street in Mount Airy. In 1971, the company moved to Lansdale and in 1999 to Hatfield. The workshop, seen here in 1925, employed skilled carvers for the carousel horses. Note the pile of wooden blanks for horse legs in the front of the photograph. A picture of a carousel horse is on page 111. (Courtesy of Philadelphia Toboggan Coasters Inc.)

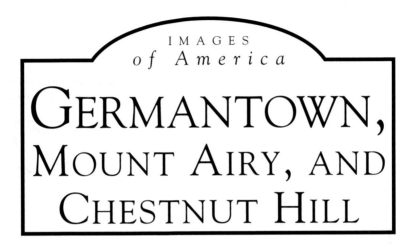

IMAGES
of America

GERMANTOWN, MOUNT AIRY, AND CHESTNUT HILL

Judith Callard
Germantown Historical Society

ARCADIA
PUBLISHING

Copyright © 2000 by Germantown Historical Society
ISBN 978-0-7385-0416-2

Published by Arcadia Publishing
Charleston SC, Chicago IL, Portsmouth NH, San Francisco CA

Printed in the United States of America

Library of Congress Catalog Card Number: 00100870

For all general information contact Arcadia Publishing at:
Telephone 843-853-2070
Fax 843-853-0044
E-mail sales@arcadiapublishing.com
For customer service and orders:
Toll-Free 1-888-313-2665

Visit us on the Internet at www.arcadiapublishing.com

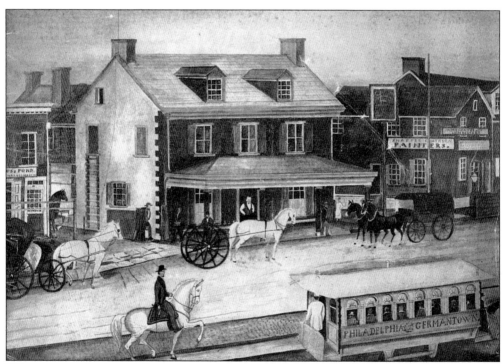

This is an artist's view of Germantown Avenue opposite the old General Wayne Hotel at the southwest corner of Germantown Avenue and Manheim Street. The horse-drawn streetcar in front indicates that the scene is after 1859. On the right is Schaeffer and Chatburn's, house and sign painters. A photograph of the hotel after it was altered can be seen on page 56.

CONTENTS

ACKNOWLEDGMENTS

Many people have helped with this book. Thanks go to the following staff, publications committee members, and volunteers at the Germantown Historical Society: Mary K. Dabney, Cynthia Gosling, Eugene Stackhouse, William Burke, James Duffin, David Moore, Irvin Miller, Millicent Hartsfield, Joan Coale, Jeffrey Wise, Heike Rass-Paulmier, and Sybil Beckett.

Special thanks to Patricia Henning for her knowledge, research companionship, and encouragement throughout.

Elizabeth Farmer Jarvis at the Chestnut Hill Historical Society was generous with her knowledge and time and always knew who to call for details of Chestnut Hill history.

Thanks to all the individuals and institutions who allowed the use of their photographs and art. Images are from the collections of the Germantown Historical Society unless otherwise credited.

The following people at local historic sites and businesses kindly shared their knowledge: Peter Lapham, Chestnut Hill Historical Society; Margo Burnette, Stenton Museum; Bob Gutowski, Morris Arboretum of the University of Pennsylvania; John Groff and Elizabeth Solomon, Wyck; Helene Weis, Willet Stained Glass Studios; Robyn Kulp, Lutheran Archives at Philadelphia; Ed MacFarland, Kirk & Nice Funeral Home; Thomas D. Rebbie, president, and William Dauphinee, vice-president, Philadelphia Toboggan Coasters Inc.; Chris Nicholson, Germantown Monthly Meeting of the Religious Society of Friends; Gordon Howard, Ebenezer Maxwell Mansion; Linda Brown and Nicki Toizer, Awbury Arboretum; Ruth Cella, Pennsylvania School for the Deaf; Betty Ann Fellner, Sedgwick Cultural Center; Dennis Barnebey, Germantown High School; Katharine Minehart, Germantown Theatre Guild; Edwin Probert, Germantown Academy; Andrew A. Zellers-Frederick, Historic RittenhouseTown; Elizabeth Laurent and Anne Roller, Cliveden of the National Trust; John Alviti, Franklin Institute; Thomas Glasgow, Grumblethorpe; and Betty Shellenberger, Upsala Foundation Inc.

The 50 years of the *Germantown Crier* have been an invaluable resource, particularly Mark Frazier Lloyd and Sandra Mackenzie Lloyd's tercentenary exhibit article "Three Hundred Years of Germantown History" (*Crier* Vol. 35:1, 1983).

Rina Bander and Dee Dee Risher copyedited the captions; Robert M. Skaler shared postcards from his collection; Patricia Manley and Naomi Satchel-Strange of Settlement Music School, and James Butler provided leads; Bernice Tripp, Jefferson Moak, Sanford Sher, Justine Gerety, Jeanette Turnbull, David Contosta, and Paul McCloskey provided expertise.

Any errors are those of the writer.

Thanks to Dan, Ben, and Eliza Callard for their help throughout.

Thanks to Kerper Studio Photography Inc. of Wyndmoor and Penguin Photo of Chestnut Hill for their good service.

INTRODUCTION

The images in this book span three centuries of life in Germantown, Mount Airy, and Chestnut Hill—the neighborhoods of the city of Philadelphia that make up the old German Township. Germantown was founded by German-speaking immigrants in 1683 and was an independent township until 1854, when it was incorporated into the city of Philadelphia. The neighborhoods are linked by a road that follows the path of a Lenni Lenape trail. Once known as the Great Road or the Germantown Road, it was known as Main Street in the early 20th century and as Germantown Avenue today. The linear pattern of Germantown's settlement along this road is distinctive. In the Revolutionary War, Germantown was the site of the 1777 Battle of Germantown. In the 1860s, two Civil War hospitals—Mower General Hospital in Chestnut Hill and Cuyler Hospital—served thousands of wounded soldiers. Germantown Avenue is a "living laboratory" of Germantown history, preserving four centuries of architectural styles, and is itself designated a National Historic Landmark.

Before Europeans came, the Lenni Lenape fished and hunted in the Wissahickon Valley. European settlers drew on the creek and forest for wood, stone, and industrial energy. They also praised its beauty in poetry and art. Today, it is a popular recreation area, serving hikers, birdwatchers, fishermen, cyclists, and horse riders. The valley's beautiful stream is designated a National Natural Landmark.

Leaving Europe for religious freedom and economic opportunity, early settlers began to arrive in 1683. Under the leadership of Francis Daniel Pastorius, they built Germantown from the ground up—finding springs, setting up a gristmill, planting crops, creating laws and punishments, and practicing their trades. The early settlers brought many talents: Pastorius himself was a linguist and lawyer; Johannes Kelpius, a healer; Christopher Witt, a self-taught physician; William Rittenhouse, a minister and papermaker; Christopher Saur, master of many trades, including printing; and Benjamin Lay, a fiery abolitionist. Numerous linen weavers and other tradesmen brought their skills to the new settlement.

Among these early settlers were four German Quakers who, in 1688, wrote the first protest against slavery in North America and presented it to their Meeting. Although it was tabled, many Quakers were early opponents of slavery, and their presence has influenced many aspects of Germantown life. There were few African Americans in Germantown until the 20th century, but they have always had a presence in the area. By 1800, sixty free blacks and seven enslaved blacks were recorded as living in Germantown.

Other significant people connected with Germantown include George Washington, who stayed at the Deshler-Morris House for periods in 1793 and 1794; artists Gilbert Stuart and Charles Willson Peale; Louisa May Alcott and her parents—Bronson, an educational reformer, and Abigail, an early member of the Female Anti-Slavery Society in Philadelphia; botanist

Margaretta Morris; actors Fanny Kemble and Charlotte Cushman; Renaissance men such as Reuben Haines; and a host of others.

With the beginnings of industrialization in the early 19th century, large numbers of immigrants came to work in the factories and textile mills. Most residents worked in these mills or in trades as tanners, carpenters, and hat makers. By the mid-19th century, steam power had largely replaced waterpower, allowing expansion of the factories and mills. One of the first railroads in America—the Philadelphia, Germantown, and Norristown line—was built as far as Germantown in 1832. A railroad line to Chestnut Hill opened in 1854, the same year that the German Township became part of Philadelphia.

With the railroads came garden suburbs as wealthy businessmen began to build estates in Germantown, Mount Airy, and Chestnut Hill. Railroad and coach service increased the development of northern Chestnut Hill in the mid-1850s, and in the late 1870s, Henry Howard Houston, a railroad magnate living in Germantown, began his purchase of more than 3,000 acres in Chestnut Hill. The completion of the Pennsylvania Railroad on the west side of these communities in 1884 was pushed by Houston and benefited his business greatly. With his son-in-law George Woodward, he built a planned community of hundreds of housing units for the up-and-coming middle class. They rented rather than sold these units, thus controlling who lived in the neighborhood and how it was developed.

At the end of the 19th century, the population was increasing so rapidly that space was at a premium, particularly in Germantown. Large estates were subdivided for apartment buildings and houses. New schools had to be built. Farsighted people such as Thomas Meehan, horticulturalist and councilman, pushed for the creation of green spaces, including Vernon Park.

Throughout Germantown's history, there has been a strong strain of charitable activity, much of it through the churches. Many groups started relief societies, organizations to keep working men and women off the streets and out of the taverns, homes for orphans and the indigent, free medical care, and free libraries. They were inspired to help poor youths become good citizens through organizations such as the YMCA, the YWCA, and other clubs. The clubs were routinely segregated by race and sex until the mid-20th century.

Today, many residents of Germantown, Mount Airy, and Chestnut Hill see their neighborhoods as separate communities, each with their own characteristics. There is no Germantown and Chestnut Hill Improvement Association as there was in the early 20th century, and the neighborhoods are no longer united as the 22nd Ward. However, they are linked by a desire to see their historic sites preserved and visited both by residents of the community and tourists. Twelve historic houses, as well as the Awbury and Morris Arboretums and the Chestnut Hill Historical Society, are open to the public.

The Germantown Historical Society, founded in 1900, is one of the oldest local historical societies in the United States. It has an extensive collection of artifacts and research materials. Its mission is to preserve, protect, and interpret Germantown's rich and diverse history for residents and visitors. The historical society believes that understanding the past gives us insight for the future and promotes pride in the community today.

Bibliography

Contosta, David. *Suburb in the City: Chestnut Hill, Philadelphia, 1850–1990.* Ohio State University Press, 1992.

———. *A Philadelphia Family: The Houstons and Woodwards of Chestnut Hill.* University of Pennsylvania Press, 1988.

Webster, Richard. *Philadelphia Preserved: Catalog of the American Buildings Survey.* Temple University Press, 2nd edition 1981.

West, Sarah. *Rediscovering the Wissahickon Through its Science and History.* Westford Press, 1993.

Wolf, Stephanie Grauman. *Urban Village: Population, Community, and Family Structure in Germantown, Pennsylvania 1683–1800.* Princeton University Press, 1976.

One

THE FOUNDING OF GERMANTOWN

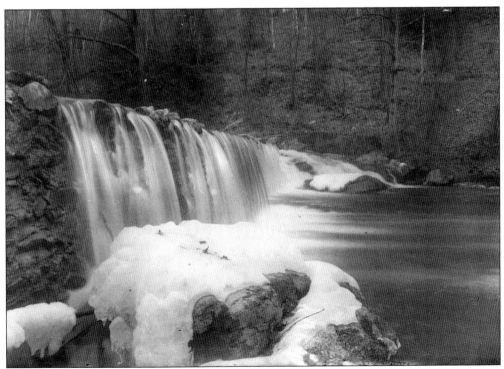

The beauty of the Wissahickon gorge has inspired mystics, writers, and artists for over three centuries. Native Americans lived in these forests for thousands of years, farming the ridge and fishing and hunting in the gorge. The Lenni Lenape tribe gave the river the name *Wissahickon*, which is thought to mean "catfish creek." For more than 200 years, it provided stone, wood, and industrial energy to European settlers.

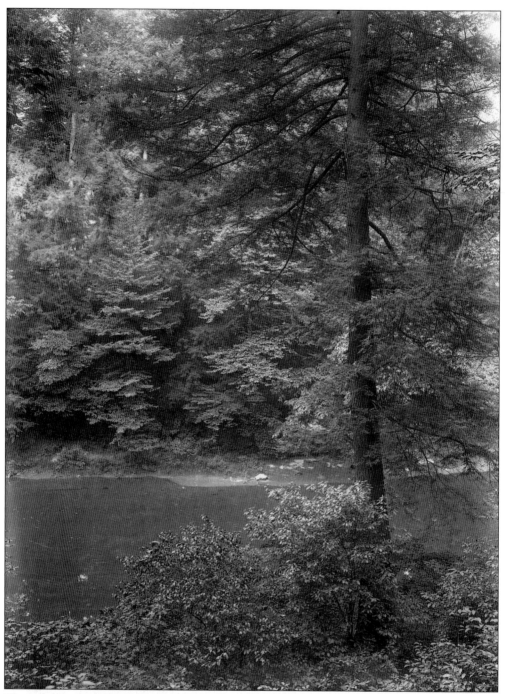

"Es ist alles nur Wald" ("All is forest"), wrote Francis Daniel Pastorius, the founder of Germantown. He directed this comment in 1683 to a group of Germans in Frankfurt who, encouraged by William Penn, were planning to emigrate to Pennsylvania. A later visitor described the trees of the thick forest as "oak, chestnut, walnut, locust, apple, hiccory [sic], blackberry bushes." William Penn's dealings with the Lenni Lenape were friendly, but his goal was to settle Europeans on the land.

This granite statue, often referred to as Tedyuscung, was erected in the Wissahickon Woods in 1902 as a tribute to the Lenni Lenape ("original people") who lived on the land that became the German Township. Francis Daniel Pastorius wrote that the Lenape "have accepted a sum of money from William Penn and have withdrawn very far away from us, into the wild forest, where they support themselves by the chase, shooting birds and game, and also by catching fish. They exchange their elk and deer-skins, beaver, martin, and turkeys for powder, lead, blankets, and brandy."

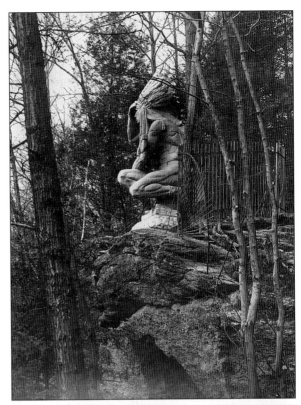

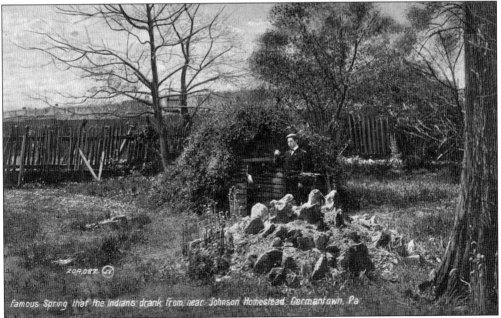

Famous Spring that the Indians drank from, near Johnson Homestead, Germantown, Pa.

There was contact between the Lenni Lenape and the European settlers until the mid-18th century. Native Americans sometimes camped in large numbers at James Logan's house, Stenton. This spring behind the Johnson house at Washington Lane and Germantown Avenue provided water to both Native Americans and Europeans.

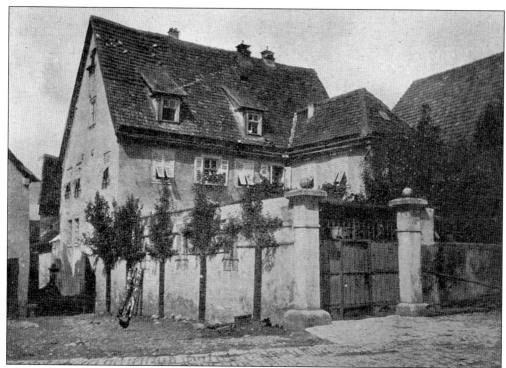

Francis Daniel Pastorius, a devout and scholarly man, was born in this house in Sommerhausen, Germany. In 1683, he arrived in Philadelphia County with others. A few months later, a group from Krefeld, Germany, arrived and, under his leadership, drew lots for land in the 5,700-acre tract that became known as the German Township. Pastorius wanted to lead "a quiet, godly life in a howling wilderness—a heavy task to perform among the bad examples and numberless [vanities] in Europe."

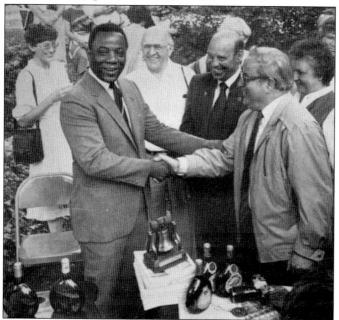

Philadelphia mayor W. Wilson Goode is seen greeting the mayor of Sommerhausen (the birthplace of Francis Daniel Pastorius) and members of the Bavarian State Parliament during their 1984 visit to Germantown.

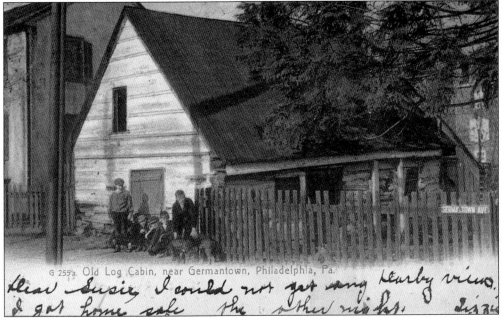

G 255 a. Old Log Cabin, near Germantown, Philadelphia, Pa.

Hear Susie I could not get any Nearby view. I got home safe the other night. Lizzie

Some of the early settlers, including Francis Daniel Pastorius, lived in cave dwellings in Philadelphia until they could build in Germantown. They built log cabins or sod huts along a 2-mile stretch of a Native American trail, which is now Germantown Avenue. Christopher Yeakel, a German cooper, built this cabin in 1743 on Germantown Avenue at Mermaid Lane, where it stood until 1909.

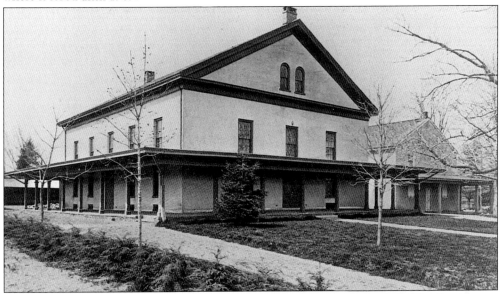

A Quaker Meeting was formed soon after the German immigrants arrived. The Friends met first at members' houses and then probably in a log structure at Germantown Avenue and what is now Coulter Street. In 1690, Jacob Shoemaker donated land on the same site, and a stone meetinghouse was erected in 1705. This unusual view shows two meetinghouses, one built in 1812 and the other in 1867. The old one, on the right, was demolished a few years later. (Courtesy of Germantown Monthly Meeting of the Religious Society of Friends.)

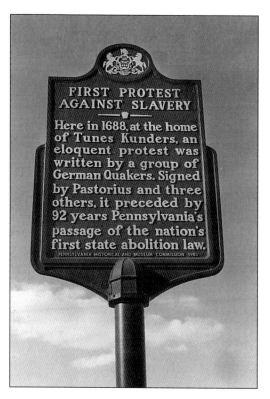

FIRST PROTEST
AGAINST SLAVERY
▼
Here in 1688, at the home
of Tunes Kunders, an
eloquent protest was
written by a group of
German Quakers. Signed
by Pastorius and three
others, it preceded by
92 years Pennsylvania's
passage of the nation's
first state abolition law.
PENNSYLVANIA HISTORICAL AND MUSEUM COMMISSION 1983

African Americans were present in
Germantown in small numbers from the
beginnings of settlement. In 1688, a group
of German Quakers met, probably at the
house of dyer Thones Kunders, and wrote
the first protest against slavery in North
America. Francis Daniel Pastorius, Garret
Hendricks, and Derick and Abraham Op
den Graeff signed the passionate protest,
which demanded of their fellow Quakers,
"Have these [people] not as much right to
fight for their freedom as you have to keep
them slaves?" The protest reached Yearly
Meeting but was tabled. A commemorative
marker stands near the site of the signing at
Germantown Avenue and Wister Street.

Many of the first
settlers were linen
weavers. By 1698,
Germantown had its
own seal, court, and
council. Francis Daniel
Pastorius's design for the
seal shows a grapevine, flax
blossom, and weaver's spool
"to show that the people of the
place live from grapes, flax, and
trade." Sigillum Germanopolitanum
means "little seal of the German city."

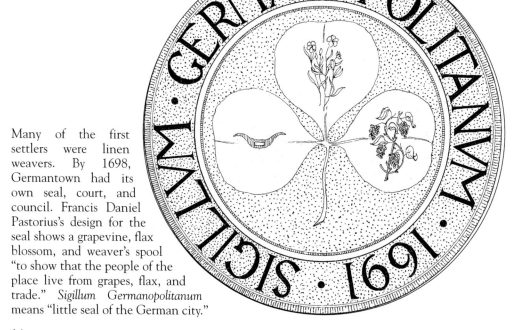

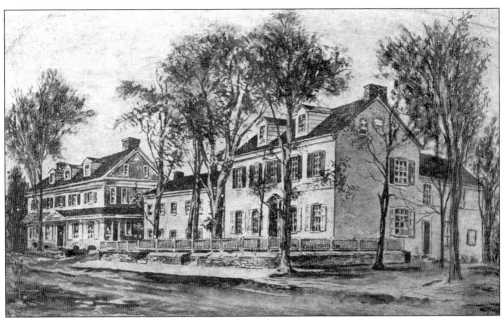

Francis Daniel Pastorius's house, shown above at center, was torn down in 1860. The house on the left, for many years the Green Tree Tavern, was built in 1748 by Pastorius's grandson and is now the church office for the First United Methodist Church of Germantown. It was made of very large timbers with hand-split oak laths and fastened with handmade nails. Over the doorway is a quotation from Virgil, which Pastorius had written above the door of his cave house: *"Parva domus, sed amica bonus; Procul est Profani"* ("A little house, but a friend of the good; keep away ye profane"). The house on the right was built by Pastorius's great-grandson. In 1898, its owner, Dr. William Rush Dunton, allowed it to be moved around the corner to 25 East High Street so that the church could be built. The photograph below shows the house being moved.

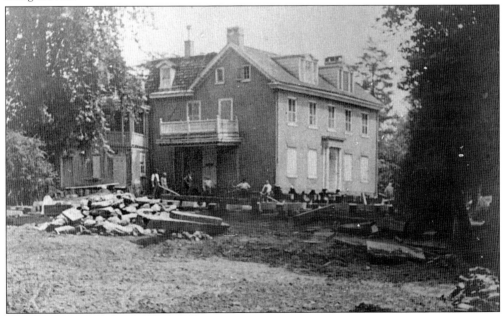

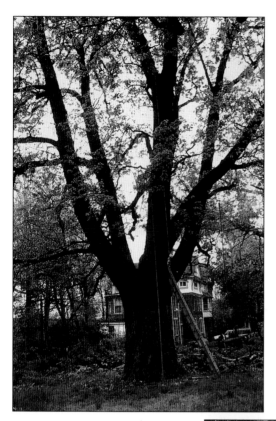

This giant chestnut oak (*Quercus prinus*) in Howell Park behind the Germantown post office is probably 300 years old. It is 94 feet tall with a circumference of almost 18 feet, making it one of the two largest chestnut oaks in Pennsylvania. With the help of neighbors and McFarland Landscape Services, it has survived lightning, ice storms, and human damage.

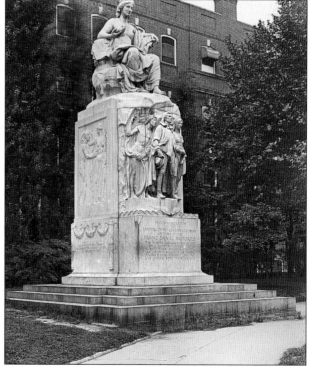

The Founders Statue in Vernon Park honors the settlers of Germantown. Designed by Albert Jaegers, it was paid for by Congress and the National German American Alliance. The statue was completed in 1917 as the United States was about to enter World War I. There were protests that the female figure represented Germany Triumphant, though the sculptor claimed she represented Civilization, the ideal of German pilgrims. Because of threats against the statue it was encased in a box until 1920 and then quietly dedicated.

Two

THE GERMAN TOWNSHIP

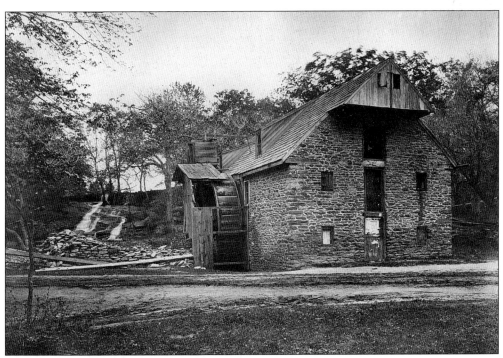

As soon as Germantown was laid out, all the basic services were needed. Richard Townsend built a gristmill on Mill Street (now Church Lane) at the edge of Germantown to provide flour for the settlers. Later, it was known as Lukens Mill and then Roberts Mill. It was torn down *c.* 1873. Millers became some of the wealthiest residents of Germantown.

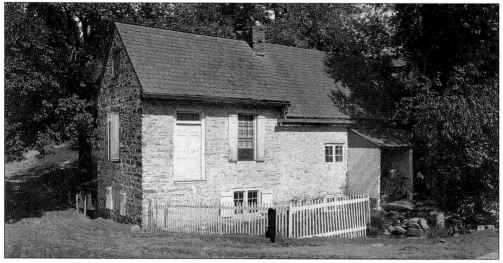

Another pressing need in the new township was paper. In 1690, William Rittenhouse, a German papermaker and Mennonite minister, built the first paper mill in America on the Monoshone Creek. Until *c.* 1710, the mill provided all the American-made paper used by Philadelphia and New York printers. It made about 1,000 sheets of paper every day, which was a very small percentage of what the colonies needed (the rest had to be imported). Known as Historic RittenhouseTown, the National Historic Landmark site in Fairmount Park is open to the public for papermaking and other programs. The Rittenhouse homestead is shown here.

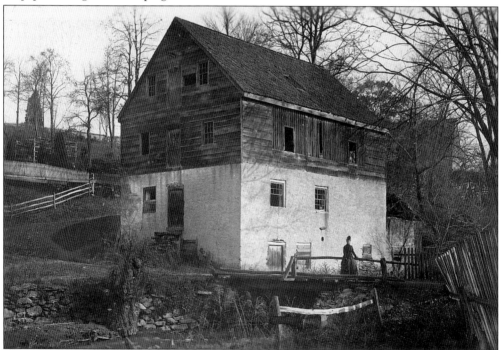

Rittenhouse's mills were built on the creek close to the homestead. Rags from the linen trade of Germantown were brought to the mill along what would become Rittenhouse Street. A poem of 1692 noted that "From linen rags good paper doth derive / The first trade keeps the second trade alive." Shown is the third Rittenhouse mill in 1890.

18

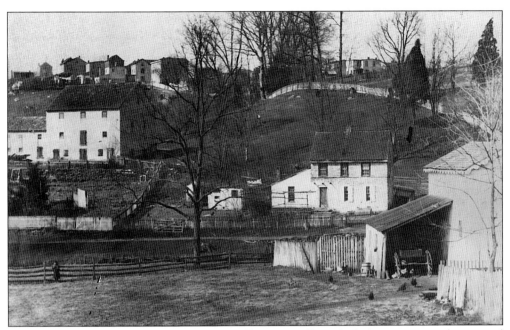

By the mid-1800s, other paper mills, as well as sawmills and cloth processing plants, used waterpower. RittenhouseTown became a thriving industrial village of more than 40 structures, including a school, firehouse, Baptist church, and workers' houses. This view looks north to Blue Bell Hill.

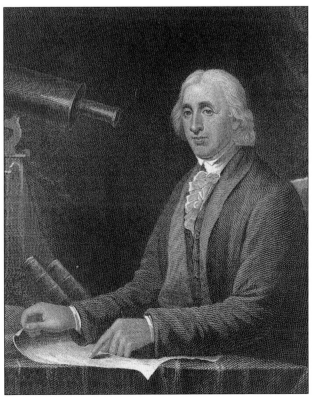

The Rittenhouse homestead was the birthplace of David Rittenhouse in 1732. He was a self-taught astronomer, clockmaker, scholarly writer, second president of the American Philosophical Society, state treasurer, and director of the U.S. Mint. The family moved to a farm in Montgomery County when he was young. Before the Revolutionary War, he surveyed the boundaries of Pennsylvania and during the war, he was an engineer.

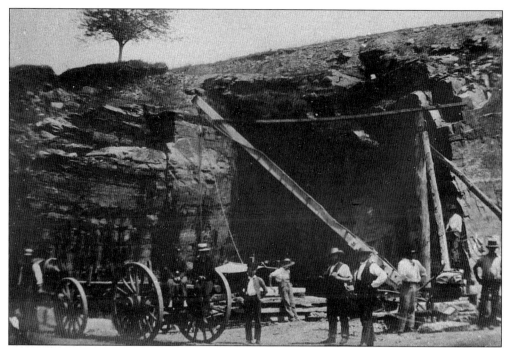

The last surviving RittenhouseTown industry was McKinney's quarry in the hill at the foot of what is now Alden Park Apartments. Daniel McKinney leased the hill in 1837 and worked the quarry, which specialized in high quality curbstones. Much of Philadelphia and Norristown was curbed from this quarry. The quarry was open until 1910.

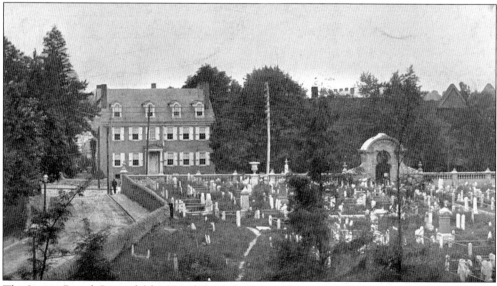

The Lower Burial Ground (the Hood Cemetery) is at Germantown Avenue and Logan Street. In 1692, one-half acre was deeded to the borough for a burial place, which was later expanded to two acres. The British officers General Agnew and Colonel Bird were buried here during the Revolutionary War but their remains were secretly moved later. The cemetery name was changed c. 1850 after William Hood paid for a wall and a marble entrance gate. More than 1,000 people are buried here, including 41 soldiers from the Revolutionary War.

Johannes Kelpius and a group of mystics who believed in magic and healing left Germany in 1694 to avoid persecution and to await the Second Coming of Christ in America. Kelpius had graduated from university at age 16 and was educated in chemistry and astronomy. The group lived near Germantown at the Wissahickon Creek, where Kelpius built a cave in the hillside for solitary reflection. Members of the community played instruments, wrote hymns, and shared their healing arts with other settlers.

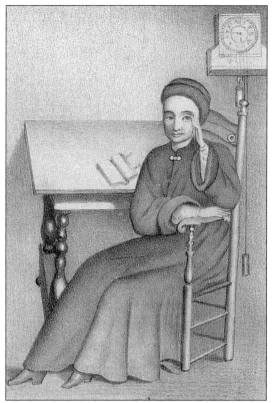

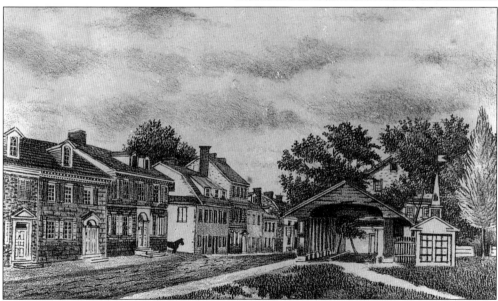

In 1704, people petitioned provincial authorities for a market at Germantown Avenue and School House Lane. A prison, stocks, and a pound were built, followed by a market house in 1741 and a firehouse in 1814. Public gatherings were held in Market Square, but the market itself was apparently not a center of Germantown life. Many prominent families such as the Bringhursts, Delaplaines, Ashmeads, and Bensells lived nearby.

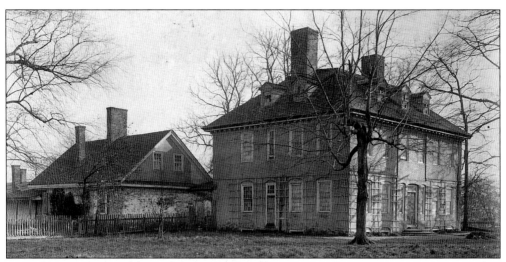

James Logan, a successful merchant, retired to his mansion, Stenton, in 1730. He served as William Penn's secretary and the Penn family agent for 50 years. In the next generation, during the Revolutionary War, Stenton was saved by an African-American servant named Dinah. When two soldiers came to burn the building, Dinah sent a troop of British soldiers after them by claiming they were deserters. This photograph was taken by Edward Sanborn in 1899.

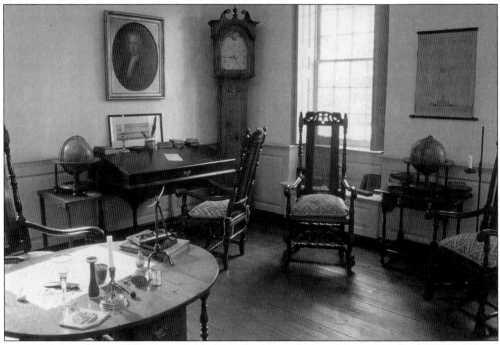

James Logan, whose office is seen here, was a serious scholar and assembled a library of Latin and Greek classics and science. The collection is now at the Library Company of Philadelphia. Logan was the first American to own Newton's *Principia Mathematica*. Thomas Godfrey, a young glazier who worked at Stenton in 1730, became interested in the refraction of light and was given access to the library. Godfrey developed the quadrant, a simple instrument for making astronomical measurements. (Courtesy of Stenton, National Society of the Colonial Dames of America/PA.)

Deborah Norris Logan was married to James Logan's grandson, Dr. George Logan. She found James Logan's invaluable correspondence with William Penn and transcribed it. She was an indefatigable gardener who grew lemon and orange trees in the greenhouse, wisteria, horse chestnuts, holly, and jasmine. She kept a remarkable journal of her life at Stenton. Stenton Museum, at Eighteenth and Windrim Streets, is open to the public. (Courtesy of Stenton, National Society of the Colonial Dames of America/PA.)

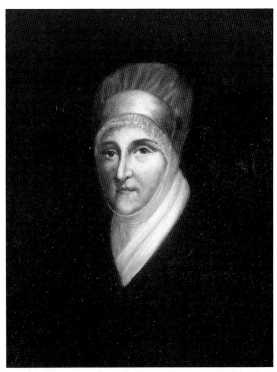

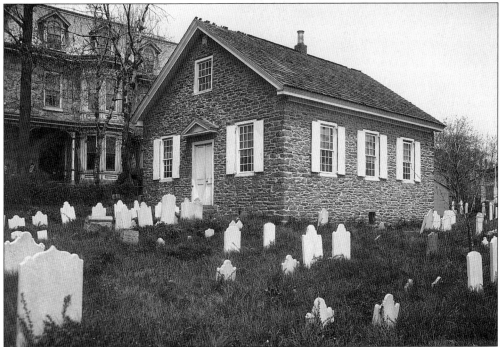

This early church was built by the Mennonites. Their 1708 log cabin meetinghouse was replaced by this stone structure in 1770. The church stands at 6121 Germantown Avenue, below Pastorius Street. Many Mennonites went beyond Germantown to find farmland. William Rittenhouse, the papermaker, was the first ordained Mennonite minister in the United States.

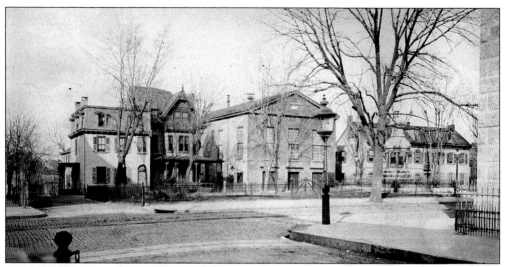

One of the earliest congregations in Germantown was the German Reformed Church, which built its first church on Market Square in the 1730s and a later one in the 1830s, seen here, center. George Washington worshiped here when he stayed across the square at Isaac Franks's house. A split between English- and German-speaking congregants led to the church becoming Presbyterian in 1856. The church on the site today was built in the late 19th century and has been occupied by the Impacting Your World Christian Center since 1996.

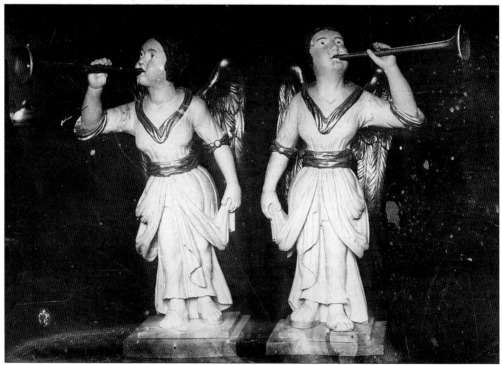

These carved wooden angels were from an 18th-century organ installed in the German Reformed Church. A trumpeting angel was attached to each side of the organ. They are now at the Germantown Historical Society. The church also has beautiful Tiffany and Godwin stained glass windows.

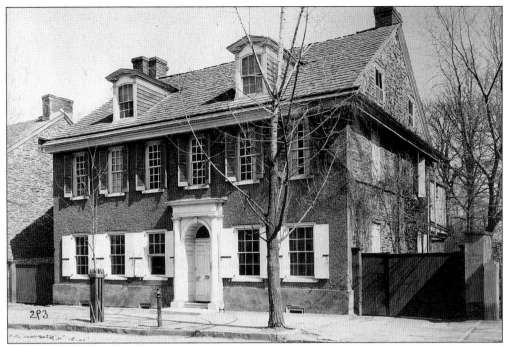

John Wister, a successful wine importer, bought a heavily forested tract on the east side of Germantown Avenue and built this Pennsylvania German-style farmhouse as a summer home in 1744. Now known as Grumblethorpe, it was home to Wister's granddaughter Sally, who recorded what she saw of the Revolutionary War in her now famous journal. British general James Agnew, fatally wounded in the Battle of Germantown, died on the parlor floor; the stain that remains there is said to be his blood. The site, which is at 5267 Germantown Avenue, is open to the public.

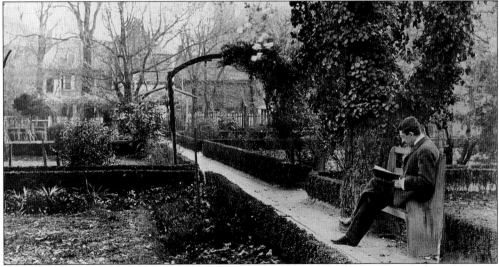

Part of John Wister's wooded tract was developed into a garden some 450 feet long and arranged in rectangles bordered by box hedges. Wister planted one of the first flowering gingko trees in the United States. Seen here sitting in the garden around the turn of the 20th century is Edwin Costley Jellett, one of Germantown's foremost historians.

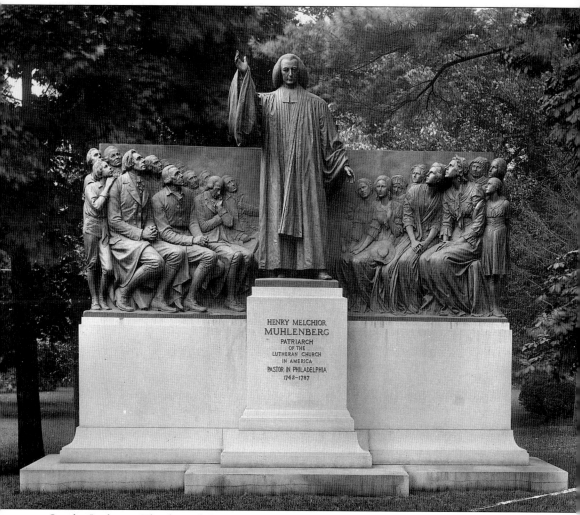

On the Lutheran Theological Seminary campus in Mount Airy is a statue of Henry Melchior Muhlenberg, who was sent from Halle, Germany, in 1742 to develop the Lutheran Church in America. He preached at St. Michael's Church and elsewhere to raise interest in Lutheranism. The sculpture, by J. Otto Schweizer (who later sculpted the "All Wars Memorial to Colored Soldiers and Sailors" in Philadelphia) depicts Muhlenberg speaking to the men and women of America. It was paid for with money raised by Lutheran Sunday-school children to celebrate the 400th anniversary of the Reformation. In 1915, the city of Philadelphia refused to give the statue a home in Fairmount Park because of anti-German sentiment, and the statue was placed at the seminary.

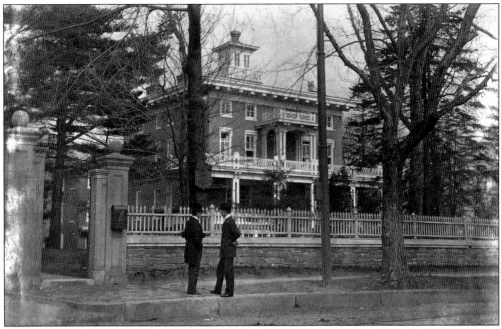

William Allen, chief justice of the Province of Pennsylvania, inherited a fortune and invested in a rum distillery, copper mine, iron furnace, and land. In 1750, Allen built a mansion, which he called Mount Airy, and settled into the life of a country gentleman, developing a large garden and driving in his landau, drawn by four coal-black horses. He was a Tory sympathizer in the Revolutionary War. In the early 1800s, Mount Airy housed the Mount Airy Seminary and later a military academy. In 1846, James Gowen razed the house and built Magnolia Villa, which is now Hagan Hall of the Lutheran Seminary (shown above before alterations were made). Below is the 1792 Joseph Miller house that was built by James Gowen's father-in-law. It was once the site of a pioneer agricultural institute and is the seminary dining room today.

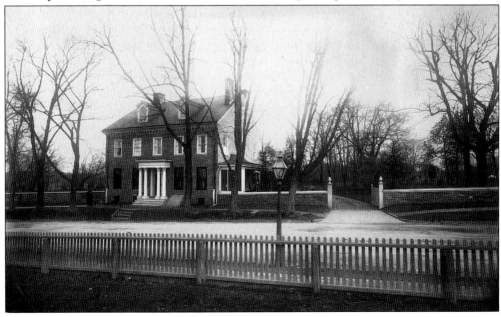

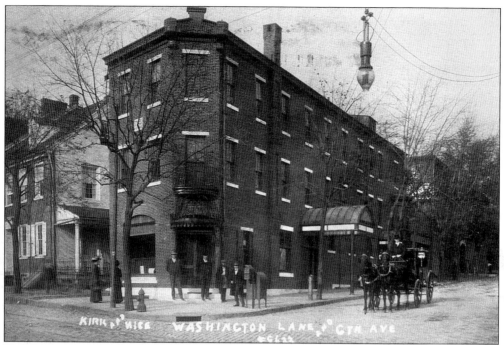

Kirk & Nice at Germantown Avenue and Washington Lane is the oldest continuously operating funeral home in the United States. It was begun by Jacob Knorr in 1761 as a cabinet shop with coffins as a sideline, but eventually moved full time into casket making. At its peak in the 1920s and 1930s, Kirk & Nice served 2,500 families every year and had 40 employees. This branch closed in 2000. (Courtesy of Robert M. Skaler collection.)

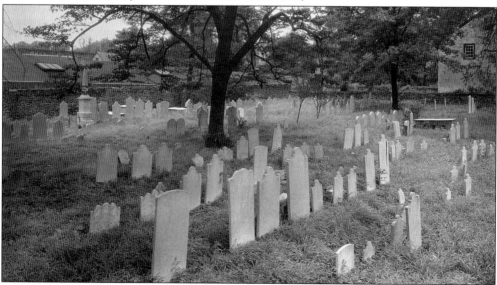

Adjacent to Kirk & Nice is the Upper Burial Ground, which was established in 1692. It was also called Ax's after its superintendent, John Frederick Ax. During the Revolutionary War, Kirk & Nice made coffins for both sides. A number of American soldiers from the Revolutionary War are buried in the cemetery, as well as soldiers from the War of 1812. There were over 1,300 burials there before it was closed.

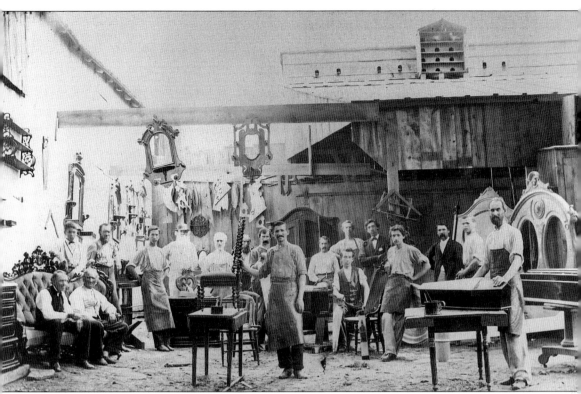

In 1812, Samuel Nice took over the business from Jacob Knorr and continued making cabinets, along with clocks, wardrobes, writing desks, and bureaus. He was joined by B. Frank Kirk and the name Kirk & Nice was adopted in 1865. By 1870, the business produced only coffins, so this picture was probably taken before that year. (Courtesy of Kirk & Nice.)

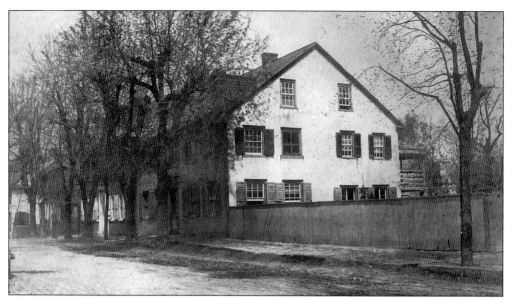

Christopher Saur's house and printing press, seen here, were on Germantown Avenue opposite Queen Lane. Saur published a German-language newspaper, and in 1742 printed the first German Bible in America (English-language Bibles were not printed in the United States until 40 years later). He charged 18 shillings for a bound copy and "for the poor and needy there is no price." His son and grandson continued the trade. Both supported the British during the Revolutionary War—an action for which their goods were seized and sold.

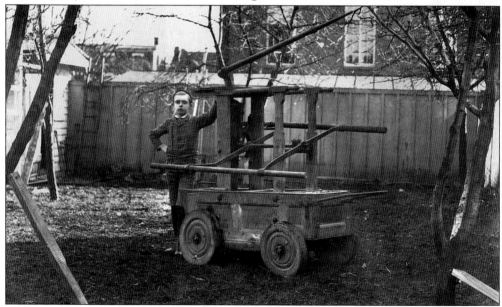

In the early days, residents were required to have two leather fire buckets in their houses and to respond to help battle fires by forming a bucket brigade from a nearby well or pond. In 1764, three fire companies were formed. In spite of divisions between German and English speakers, they united in fighting fires. One of the companies bought this hand pumper, known as Shagrag (after its English manufacturer, Newsham and Rag). It is on display at the Fireman's Hall Museum in Philadelphia.

Three

FROM GERMAN
TO ENGLISH

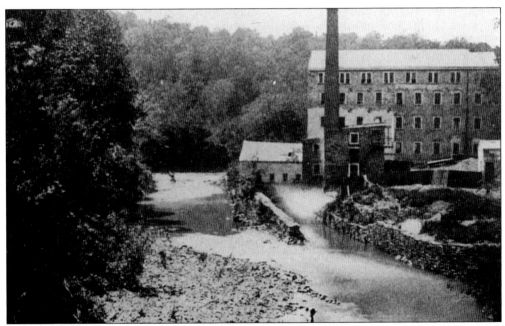

This is Kitchen's Lane mill on the Wissahickon Creek. Similar to this was Thomas Livesey's 1740s gristmill, which is thought to have been the largest in the colonies. Livesey also grew grapes and made wine; according to tradition, barrels of his wine were sunk in Devil's Pool near his house for safekeeping during the Revolutionary War. A Quaker, Livesey opposed the war and was forced to leave his home on the eve of the Battle of Germantown. The mill burned in 1793 and much wheat, flour, and salt were lost. The mill was so essential, however, that it was rebuilt immediately. By the 1830s, there were few gristmills on the Wissahickon. The Livesey house still stands and is now the home of the Valley Green Canoe Club.

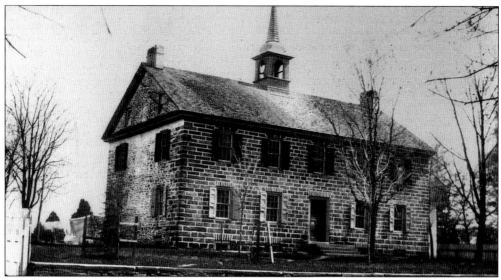

In 1759, a group met at the Green Tree Tavern to form a new school, and in 1761 opened the Union School (later called Germantown Academy). The school is seen here in 1859. Classes were conducted separately for English and German students under David Dove and Hilarius Becker. In its second year, 60 students were enrolled in the German school and 70 in the English school. By *c.* 1810, however, the separate German department was dropped, one sign of the lessening of German dominance in the township. In 1966, the school completed a move to Fort Washington.

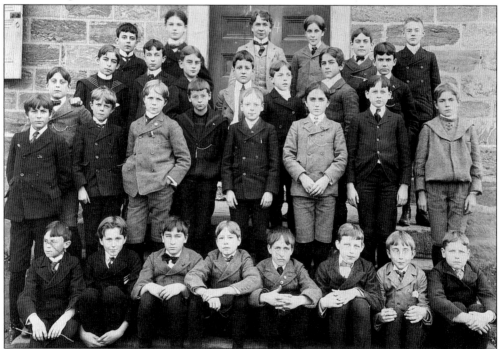

These Germantown Academy students are seen *c.* 1896. The school was led by headmaster William Kershaw for 36 years starting from 1877. Under his leadership, sports, publications, and academics flourished.

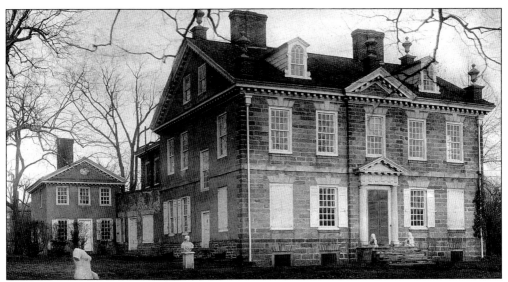

Cliveden, seen here *c.* 1900, is an outstanding example of Georgian domestic architecture and is the site of the main skirmish in the Battle of Germantown. It was completed in 1767 for Benjamin Chew, who in 1774 became chief justice of the Province of Pennsylvania. It is a National Historic Landmark and the only mid-Atlantic site of the National Trust for Historic Preservation. It is open to the public.

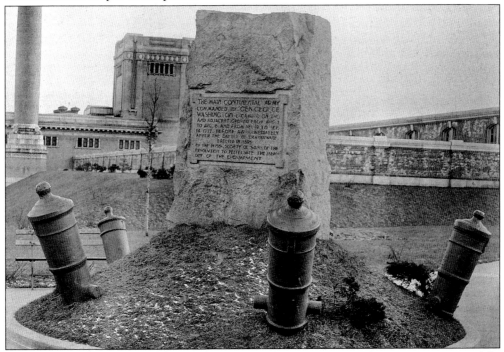

This monument is at the site where George Washington's Continental Army troops camped for a week in August 1777 and again that September before and after the Battle of Brandywine. After a visit, Lafayette reported that he found 11,000 men there who were ill armed and poorly clothed. Washington used Carlton, a nearby mansion, as his headquarters. The site, which is at Queen Lane and Fox Street, was flooded by the Queen Lane reservoir.

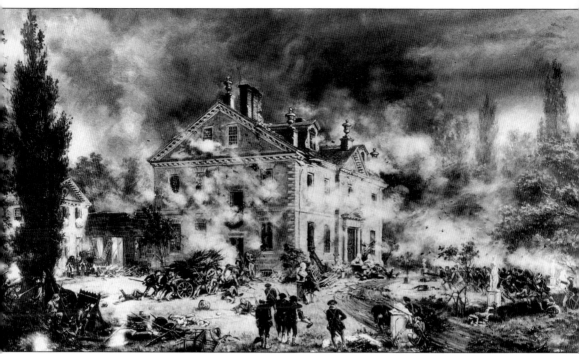

The Battle of Germantown took place on October 4, 1777. George Washington and 3,000 of his troops marched down Germantown Avenue from what is now the Lutheran Seminary in Mount Airy. They were lightly armed and unprepared to siege the house. Unable to dislodge Colonel Musgrave's 120 men from Cliveden, they suffered many casualties in the attempt and retreated through Chestnut Hill. This was the last time Washington lost a battle that he had personally led. The house was seriously damaged by cannon balls and battering rams, but the thick stone walls held. This 1874 painting of the battle by Edward Lamson Henry was commissioned by the Chew family. (Courtesy of Cliveden of the National Trust.)

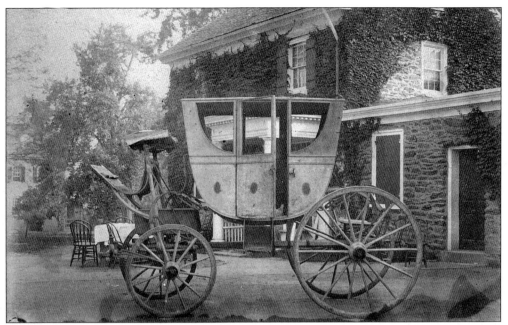

Benjamin Chew refused to support the Revolutionary War and was interned by Congress in 1777. He sold Cliveden after the war and lived for a time in Delaware. He later took an oath of allegiance to the new government and in 1791 became the president judge of the High Court of Errors and Appeals. In 1797, he repurchased Cliveden and the family held it until 1971, when they transferred it to the National Trust for Historic Preservation. His coach, seen here, was one of the finest vehicles in Philadelphia. It survived at Cliveden until a fire in 1970.

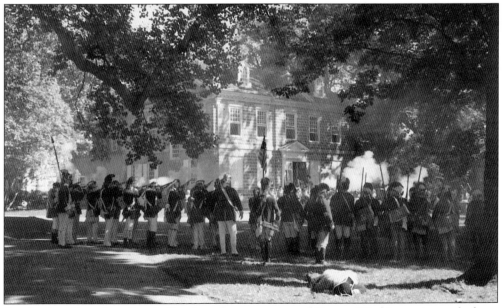

On the first Saturday of each October, the re-creation of George Washington's march down Germantown Avenue and the attack on Cliveden during the Battle of Germantown draws enthusiastic crowds. For many years, the event has been sponsored by Asher's Candies, a longtime Germantown chocolate maker. (Courtesy of Jeffrey Wise.)

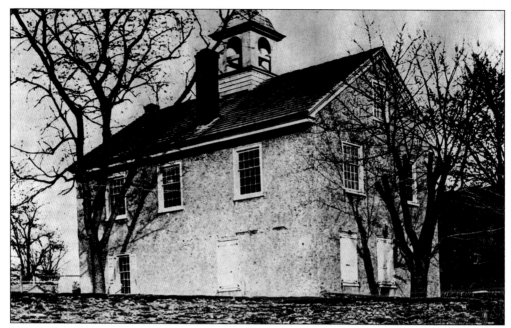

Upper Germantown residents found it hard to get their children to the Union School (Germantown Academy) since the Germantown Road was often impassable. They also wanted an English-speaking school. In 1775, a group met and founded the Concord School next to the Upper Burial Ground. As the war progressed, the school closed. However, it reopened in 1783, and a second story was added in 1819. Students used slates, slate pencils, quill pens, and ink made from nutshells and rusty nails. It is now open to the public as a museum.

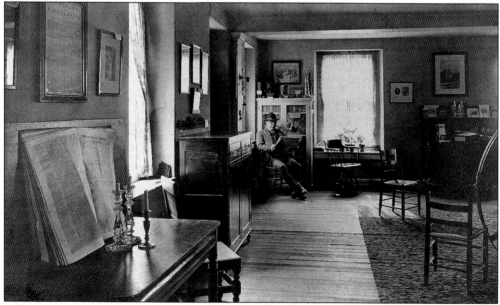

In later years, the Concord School was used extensively by local organizations, including Masonic groups, singing societies, the Germantown Hose Company, the Charter Oak Library (for more than 50 years), and as a polling place. It is seen here when it was the home of the Site and Relic Society, the original name of the Germantown Historical Society.

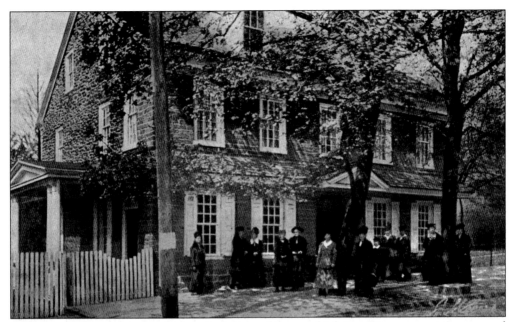

A National Historic Landmark site, the Johnson House, which is at Germantown Avenue and Washington Lane, is northwest Philadelphia's only documented station on the Underground Railroad that is operated as a museum. The German colonial farmhouse was built by a Quaker family in 1768. It stood in the thick of the Battle of Germantown and, many years later, sheltered fugitive slaves on their way north. After 1917, the Woman's Club of Germantown (seen here) occupied the house.

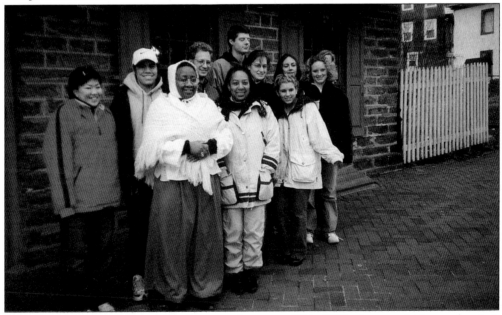

The Johnson House is a site of pilgrimage for many. This 1999 photograph shows the site's administrator, Jacqueline Wiggins (in costume) with a group from the United Campus Ministry of Western Michigan University in front of the historic Underground Railroad building. The group was in Philadelphia to study urban issues.

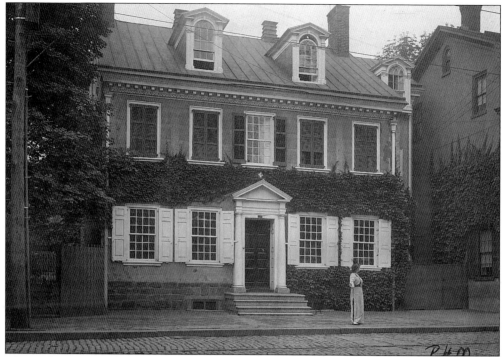

The Deshler-Morris House at 5442 Germantown Avenue was built c. 1772 by Quaker merchant David Deshler. When George Washington rented it in the fall of 1793 to avoid the yellow fever epidemic in Philadelphia, and again the following summer, it was owned by Col. Isaac Franks. Franks had fought against the British with Washington in 1776 and had escaped British captivity. Washington presided over meetings here with his divided cabinet. The Morris family owned the house for over 100 years and donated the site to the National Park Service in 1948. It is open to the public.

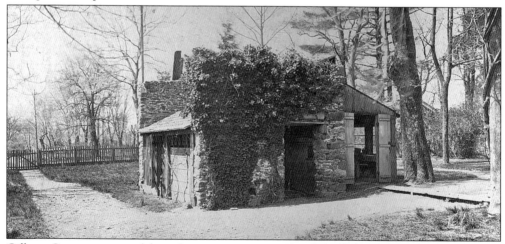

Gilbert Stuart was a celebrated portrait painter who left Philadelphia for the quiet of Germantown. He rented a house in 1796 at 5140 Germantown Avenue (now demolished) and worked in a small barn in the back of the house. George Washington recorded a visit to the studio and may have sat for a full-length portrait here. Fire ruined this barn in 1854, but the walls remained until c. 1890.

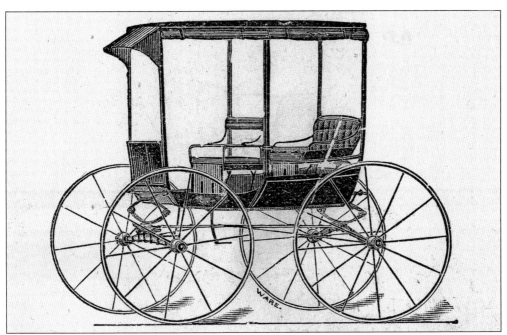

The Germantown wagon was invented soon after the Revolutionary War by the Ashmead and Bringhurst families as an alternative to the Conestoga wagon. The huge Conestogas carried flour, furs, produce, and skins to trade for hardware, sugar, coffee, tea, and shoes. The teamsters preferred to trade in Chestnut Hill or Germantown in order to avoid the appalling road into Philadelphia. This led to the development of "great stores" along Germantown Road. The lighter one-horse Germantown wagon could haul produce and livestock to market and it could also be driven to church. It was seen in Germantown as late as 1930.

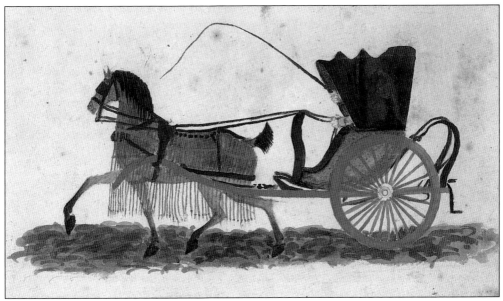

Dr. George Bensell (1757–1827) most likely drew this sketch of his carriage as a gift for his friend Charles Jones Wister Sr. An intelligent, agreeable man, Bensell liked to exchange sketches and poems with friends.

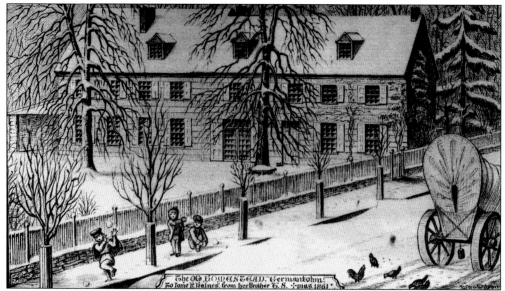

This charming view of Wyck was drawn by Thomas Stewardson for Christmas 1861. The property was first owned by Hans Millan, a German Quaker, in 1689. Nine generations of the Haines family lived there from 1689 to 1973.(Courtesy of Wyck Association.)

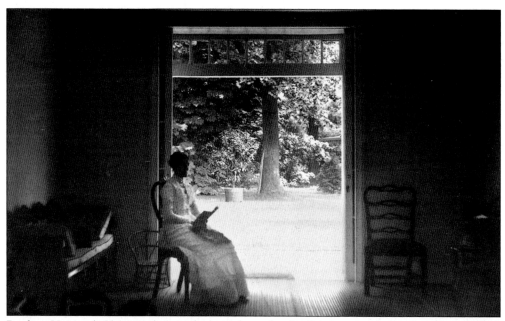

Reuben Haines (1786–1831) retired young from the family's brewing business and turned his attention to farming at Wyck. He raised animals and bees and grew fruit, corn, buckwheat, hay, and flax. He was a school reformer, an abolitionist, and first secretary of the Academy of Natural Sciences. In 1824, he commissioned William Strickland to redesign the interior of his house. Strickland created a suite of cross-ventilated rooms and a new conservatory, which opened onto a lawn on the south side and a garden on the north. Haines's youngest daughter, Jane Reuben Haines, is pictured c. 1900 looking toward the lawn from the conservatory. (Courtesy of Wyck Association.)

Reuben Haines's wife, Jane Bowne Haines, was also involved in education reform. She and other Quaker women started the Female Association, which opened charitable schools in New York beginning in 1801. Lucy Turpen, an African-American student at one of the schools and later a teacher, sewed this sampler for Jane Haines in 1815. It is now one of Wyck's treasures. (Courtesy of Wyck Association.)

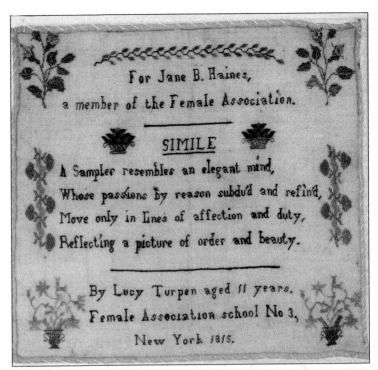

For Jane B. Haines, a member of the Female Association.

SIMILE

A Sampler resembles an elegant mind,
Whose passions by reason subdu'd and refin'd,
Move only in Lines of affection and duty,
Reflecting a picture of order and beauty.

By Lucy Turpen aged 11 years.
Female Association school No 3,
New York 1815.

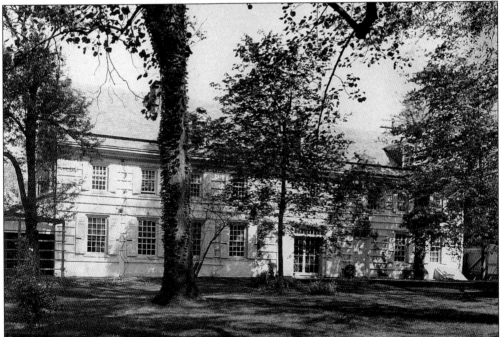

The Haines's house, seen here c. 1900, looks much the same today. Both the house and gardens are open to the public. The box-bordered rose garden was originally an 18th-century garden of fruit and vegetables, but was redesigned early in the 19th century by Jane Haines, who planted over 20 varieties of roses. There are now 37 types of old-fashioned roses. (Courtesy of Wyck Association.)

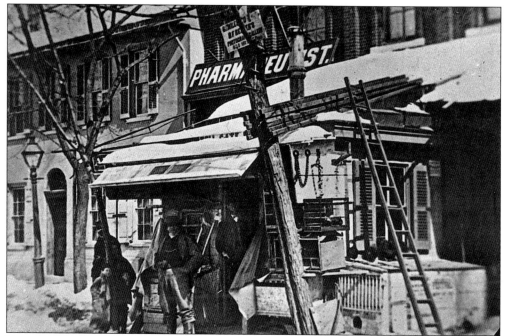

To improve the famously bad Germantown Road, the Germantown-Perkiomen Turnpike Company built a new surface in 1801. It was crudely made of chunks of stone that were covered with dirt. From 1801 to 1870, tolls were collected here at Rittenhouse Street. Enos Springer, the last toll keeper, ran a general store in what an observer called this "disgraceful shack." Tolls were 6¢ for a score of sheep, 12¢ for a two-horse coach, and 18¢ per horse for sleighs.

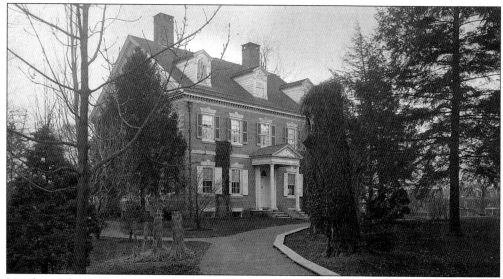

Upsala, an elegant Federal-style mansion, was built by John Johnson, the grandson of the builder of the Johnson House, in the 1790s. The land on which it stands had been owned by the family since 1766. The house is noted for its dressed stone in front, marbled steps up to a columned portico, and decorative wood carvings. Washington's troops camped here during the Battle of Germantown. Upsala is open to the public.

42

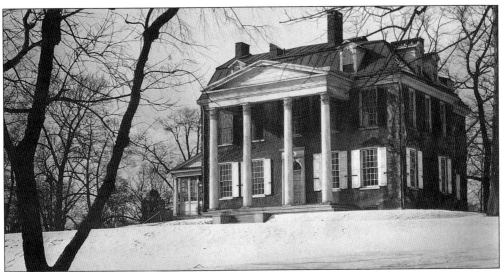

Standing at the top of Negley's Hill (the old name for the lower part of Germantown Avenue), Loudoun was built c. 1801 in the Federal style by Thomas Armat. Maria Dickinson Logan, the last owner of Loudoun, said that on a clear day she could see ships on the Delaware River from the house. When she died in 1939, she left a treasure trove: diaries, dresses, parasols, loaded rifles, stoves, lamps, as well as the house itself. A fire has since forced Loudoun to close to the public.

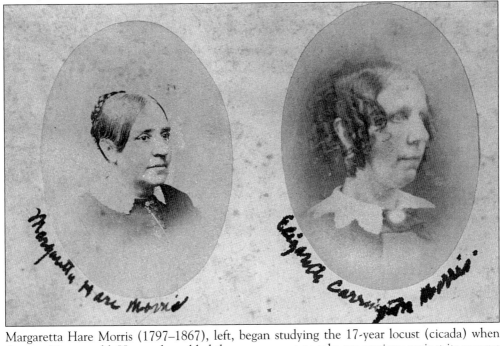

Margaretta Hare Morris (1797–1867), left, began studying the 17-year locust (cicada) when she was 20 years old. Her work enabled the government to take precautions against its ravages on crops. She also studied the raspberry pest and the Hessian fly's effect on wheat. Her sister, Elizabeth Carrington Morris (1795–1865), was a botanist and her brother, Thomas, was a naturalist. They lived at the Morris-Littell house (now demolished) at Germantown Avenue and High Street.

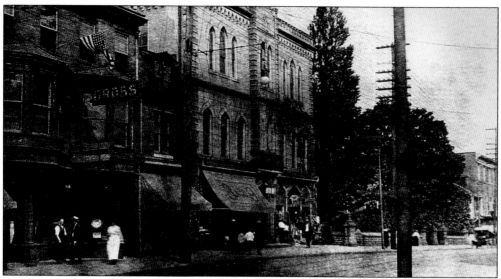

Louisa May Alcott, the author of *Little Women*, was born in a stone cottage on this site (now the Cunningham Piano Company) on November 29, 1832. Her father, Bronson, came to Germantown at the request of Reuben Haines to start a progressive school for young children. Her mother, Abigail, was a member of the Female Anti-Slavery Society of Philadelphia. The family moved to Boston when Louisa was two years old. (Courtesy of Robert M. Skaler collection.)

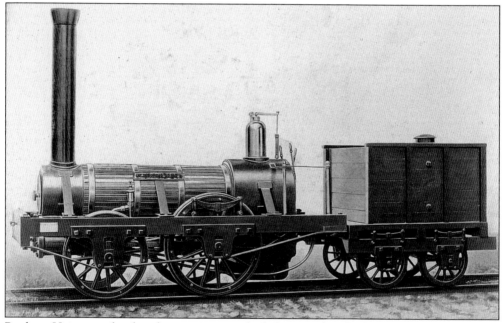

Reuben Haines and other businessmen pushed for a railroad along the eastern side of Germantown, although tavern keepers and teamsters opposed it. On June 6, 1832, the railroad opened from Philadelphia to Penn Street, the cars drawn by horses. On the first Sunday 3,000 rode the train and 30,000 came to watch. A small locomotive known as "Old Ironsides," (a replica of which is seen above) the first engine built by Mathias Baldwin, replaced horsepower in November 1832.

Four

THE INDUSTRIAL ERA BEGINS

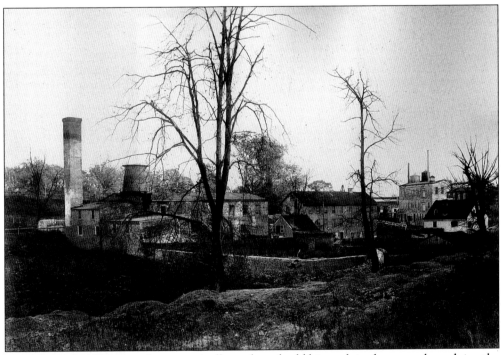

Until the early 1820s, a craftsman typically made and sold his work in the same place, doing the labor himself or with a few employees. But the advent of the railroad and steam power led to the development of dozens of factories and mills. William Logan Fisher opened his first textile mill in 1809 and, with his son Thomas, developed Wakefield Mills. They brought together skilled workers, many from England, under one roof for the large-scale manufacture of cloth and hosiery. By buying the workers' looms, the Fishers developed a monopoly.

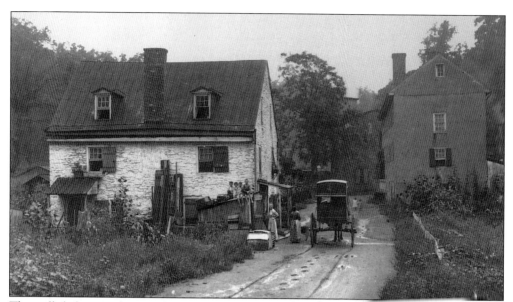

The mills led to steadier employment for the knitters but their working conditions were often harsh. Some workers lived in tenant housing such as this converted Revolutionary War powder magazine. After the turn of the 20th century, the mills fell into disrepair. The Wingohocking Creek, polluted by dyes and refuse from local mills and factories, was eventually incorporated into the sewer system. The area was bought by La Salle University in 1989 and is now their south campus.

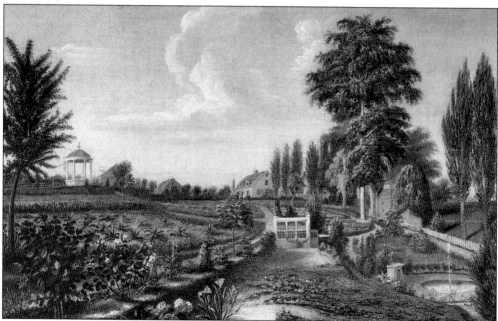

In 1810, the renowned artist Charles Willson Peale bought Belfield, a 104-acre farm with a mansion and 25 acres of woodland. He added a pool, revolving fountain, and elaborate gardens. In 1826, he sold it to his neighbor, William Logan Fisher. The mansion, a National Historic Landmark, is now part of La Salle University. This picture is Peale's own painting of the Belfield estate. (Courtesy of private collection.)

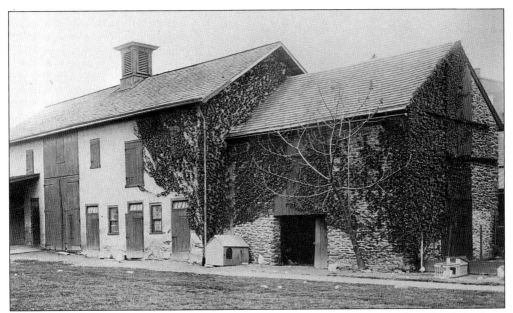

The advent of steam-powered machines changed many of the old industries. Behind this barn of the Johnson House was a tannery, which was an important source of leather for Germantown shoe and boot manufacturers until the Civil War. But the machines were the beginning of the end for hand-stitched shoes. One manufacturer, Robert Cherry, managed to survive the transformation by selling instead of making shoes.

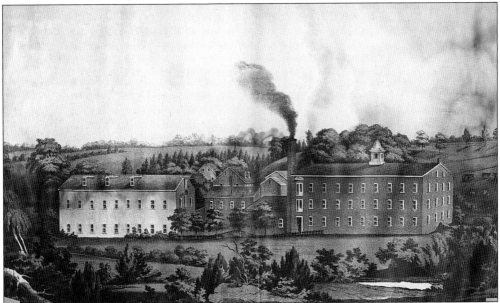

William and Andrew McCallum's Glen Echo carpet mills, founded c. 1830, were located on the Monoshone Creek at Lincoln Drive and Carpenter Lane. By the time of the Civil War, these carpets had acquired a national reputation. The factory was converted from waterpower to steam in 1835 and was expanded, eventually employing more than 100 men. Nearby was Joseph Carr's cotton yarn factory, which supplied much of its product to McCallum. In 1883, the mill moved to Wayne Junction, where it remained in business until 1898.

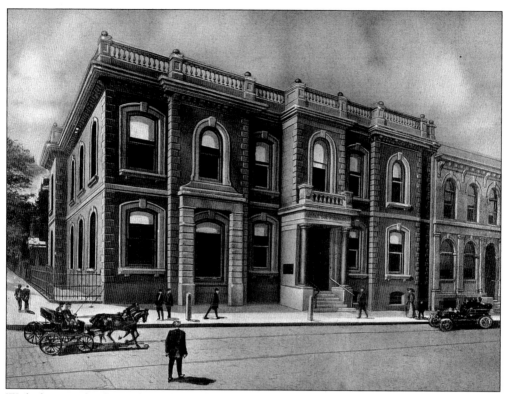

With the growth of manufacturing in the early 19th century came the need for a bank. In 1814, a group of businessmen formed the National Bank of Germantown in a house belonging to Dr. George Bensell. In 1868, it moved into a new building on Germantown Avenue at School House Lane, near the original site. Historian John Fanning Watson was the first cashier and Samuel Harvey the first president. It is now a Mellon PSFS bank.

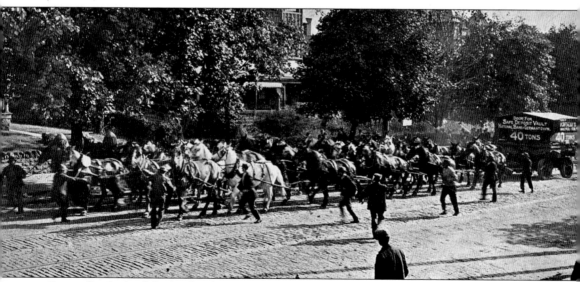

Originally, the bank had only a lockbox for security. In 1909, an addition was built to the bank and a new steel vault was brought in with much hoopla.

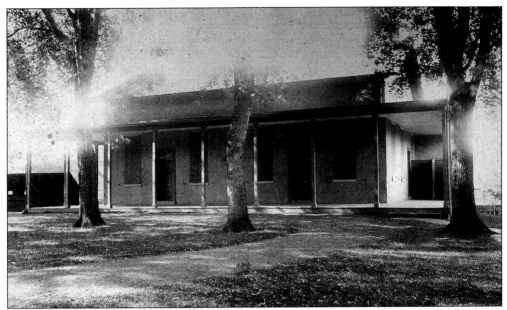

In 1827, the "Hicksite separation" in the Religious Society of Friends caused much bitterness and sorrow. Some of Elias Hicks's followers whose Meeting was on Green Street in downtown Philadelphia purchased land on School House Lane. They built the first of their meetinghouses there, keeping the name Green Street. They also started a school that is now called Greene Street Friends School.

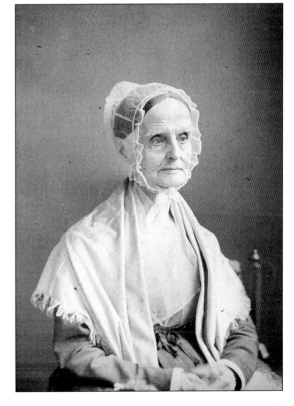

Lucretia Mott, a Quaker abolitionist, often lectured on abolition in Germantown and preached at Green Street Meeting. In November 1859, she brought John Brown's wife to the Meeting while Brown was imprisoned in Virginia after his aborted uprising at Harper's Ferry (Brown was hanged in December). When Mott died in 1880, more than 1,000 mourners followed her coffin to Fair Hill Cemetery.

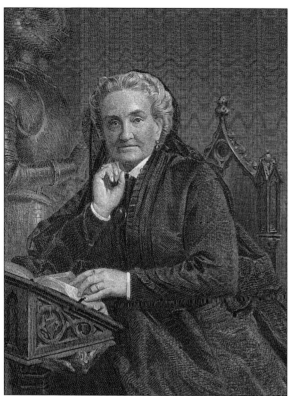

Charlotte Cushman was a famous Victorian actress who briefly managed the Walnut Street Theatre in Philadelphia in 1842. A very successful actress, she even undertook the part of Romeo. She bought the Shippen-Blair house on Germantown Avenue, which still stands. East Walnut Lane was later cut through her property.

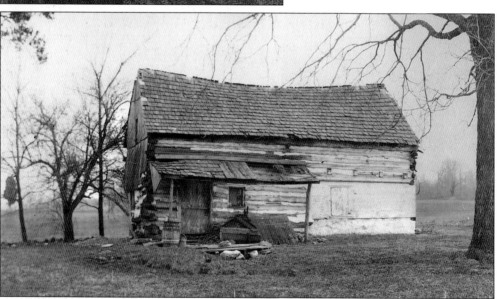

As early as 1725, James Logan suggested that Germantowners raise silkworms. In 1838 and 1839, there was a widespread silkworm craze. Cocooneries such as this one (described as "Grandmother Wolff's cocoonery") were built, and numerous mulberry trees were planted. One of the biggest was Dr. Philip Physick's Highfield Cocoonery near Morton and Haines Streets. At its height, his cocoonery had millions of silkworms. In 1840, the bottom dropped out of the silk business, and many Germantown residents lost money.

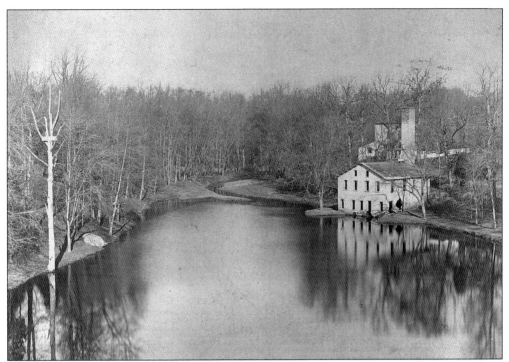

From 1851 to 1872, the Germantown Water Company pumped water from springs near Wayne Avenue and Tulpehocken Street to nearby householders via a pond. This picture of the Water Works pond was taken by J. Mitchell Elliot in 1883. In 1866, the city of Philadelphia bought the waterworks and began using water from the Schuylkill River in 1870.

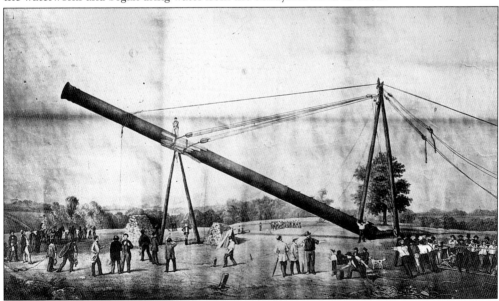

From the Water Works pond, water was pumped to a standpipe on high ground at the corner of Tulpehocken Street and Wayne Avenue. The standpipe was taken down in 1873. In Chestnut Hill, well water was pumped into a wooden tank on a stone tower at Ardleigh Street and Gravers Lane. The Water Tower remains a Chestnut Hill landmark.

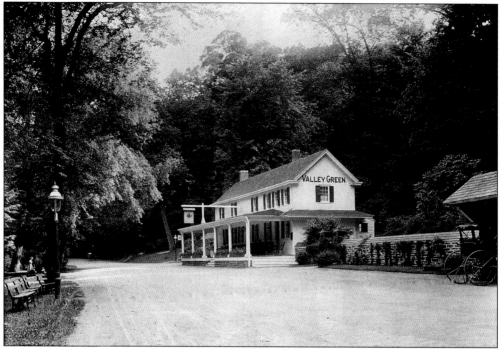

Valley Green Inn, built c. 1850 along the Wissahickon Creek, replaced previous roadhouses probably going back to Revolutionary War times. It is the last survivor of the Wissahickon Valley's inns. Today, it is a restaurant and center for the many hikers and riders who use the park. Catfish, chicken dinners, and waffles were the specialty of these inns. Diners used to arrive by carriage or sleigh, which can still be seen in the park on occasion.

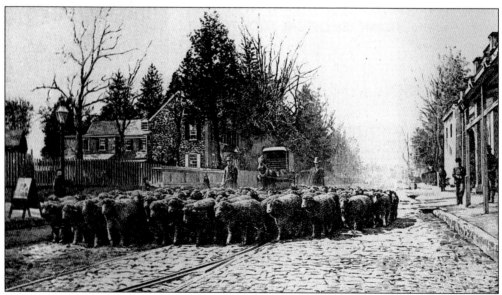

Germantown, Mount Airy, and Chestnut Hill were still somewhat rural well into the 19th century. Sheep were herded along Germantown Road, competing with Conestoga wagons and carriages. This photograph from the late 19th century was taken in Mount Airy.

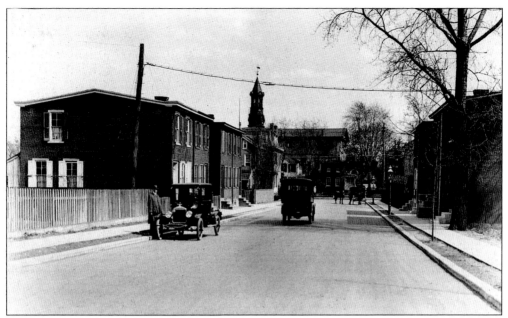

This attractive group of eight houses on McCallum Street was built c. 1855 for mill workers employed by the Wood family's lumber mill on Walnut Lane. The houses were built to persuade laborers to move from Philadelphia to rural Germantown and were eventually sold to the tenants. The houses were constructed of brick, with plain doors and no ornamentation. Inside were four boxlike rooms. The outhouses have long been demolished and the houses modernized. The original Town Hall is visible in the background.

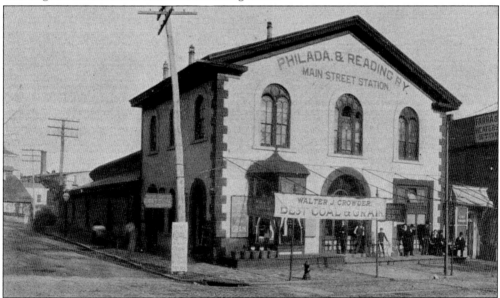

Shingle's Tavern at Germantown Avenue and Price Street served as the waiting room and ticket office for the Philadelphia, Germantown, and Norristown (PG&N) Railroad until 1855, when this depot was built. The depot continued to be used by freight, especially coal, until c. 1932, although it had been isolated when the Chestnut Hill Railroad was built. The building stood until it was destroyed by a fire in 1981.

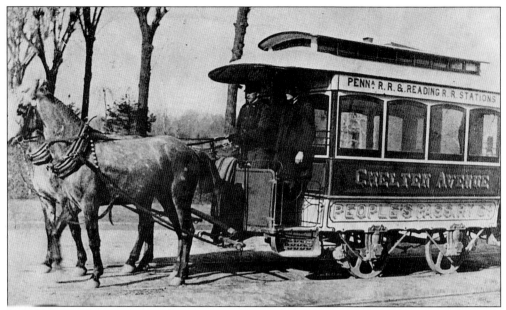

In 1859, horse-drawn streetcars began a route from Eighth Street in Philadelphia up Germantown Avenue to Phil-Ellena Street. When the first car went into service, it was decorated with flags and flowers and was pulled by four ceremonial horses. It was soon used by 2,500 people every day. This crosstown car on Chelten Avenue was added in 1892, helping to make the intersection of Germantown and Chelten Avenues the hub of Germantown's business district.

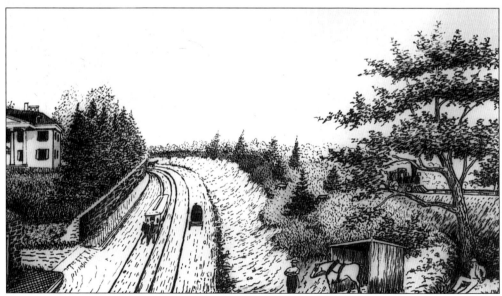

This 1863 sketch by local artist John Richards shows lower Germantown Avenue, then known as Negley's Hill, with Loudoun mansion on the left. On the right, the PG&N railroad tracks with a locomotive can be seen. A horse-drawn buggy is going up the hill while a horse-drawn streetcar comes down. At Wayne Junction, a "hill-horse" was attached to the streetcar to help pull the load up to Seymour Street. The horse then returned on its own to meet the next car.

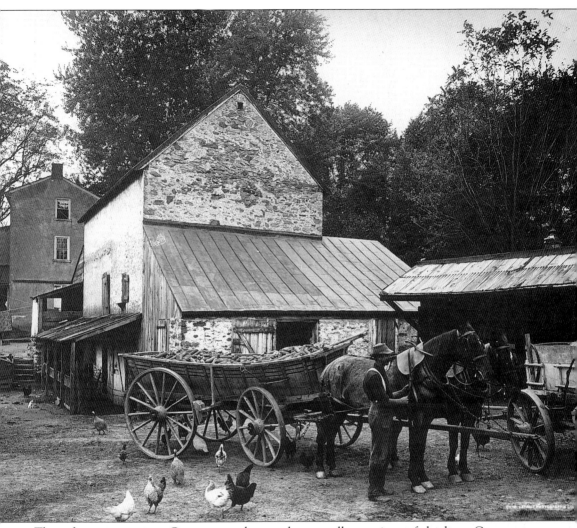

These farm wagons in a Germantown barnyard are smaller versions of the huge Conestoga wagons, which were often pulled by six to eight horses and could carry tons of produce. After the new turnpike was built in 1801, there was a great increase of traffic on Germantown Avenue. In 1812, an observer counted 500 wagons passing through Germantown in one day.

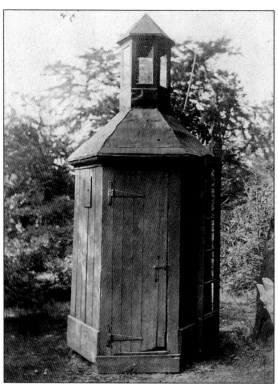

Old guard boxes such as this were used by the early constables of Germantown to house prisoners temporarily until they could be taken to jail. This one survived into the 20th century and was preserved on the grounds of John Jay Smith's house on East Penn Street. Another was housed at the Germantown Cricket Club for a number of years.

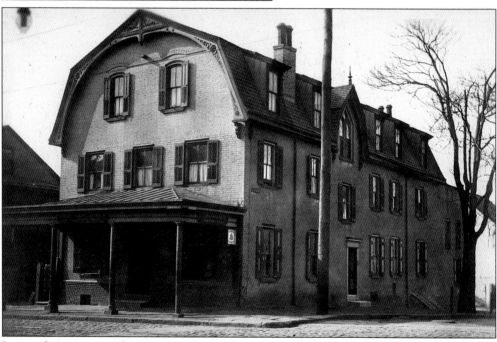

Inns and taverns served as meeting places for the community. The General Wayne Hotel, seen here, was built c. 1780 at the southwest corner of Germantown Avenue and Manheim Street. Here, many people clamored to buy stock in the PG&N railroad in 1831. The third story was added in 1866. The building is still a bar, now known as the Sugar Stick.

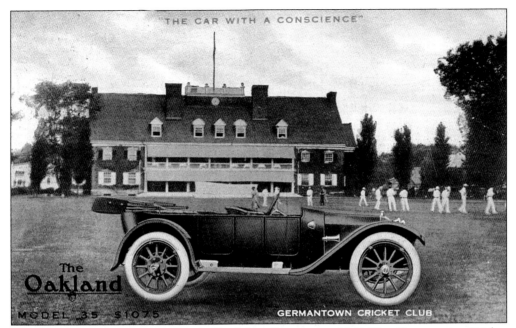

The
Oakland

MODEL 35 - $1075

GERMANTOWN CRICKET CLUB

Cricket was introduced to America by English mill workers *c.* 1844. The Germantown Cricket Club, seen here on an advertising card, was founded in 1854. It was the first cricket club in the United States. The players were taught at Belfield by William Rotch Wister. Two clubs merged at Manheim in 1889. Despite the humble origins of the game, members of the Germantown Cricket Club were mostly from upper class Germantown society.

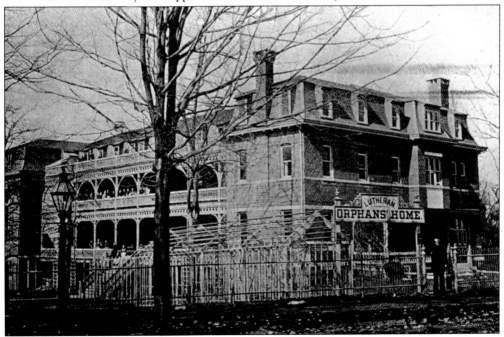

The Lutheran Orphans Home in Mount Airy opened its doors in 1859 on the site of a farm. After the Civil War, it took in many orphaned and indigent children. In 1879, another building was added for the aged and infirm. This complex is now the Germantown Home.

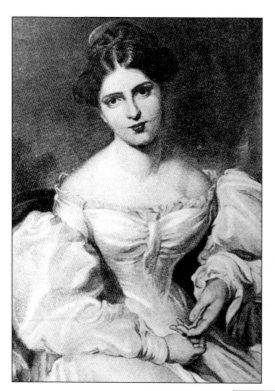

The British actress Fanny Kemble captivated America with her talent and her brilliant mind. She had many connections in Germantown and knew the town well. She described it in 1835 as having "mean-looking scattered farmhouses, and large ungainly barns, dreary in summer, desolate in winter, and absolutely void of the civilizing cheerful charms which should have belonged to it." Her marriage to a slave-owning southerner, Pierce Butler, led her to write scathing and widely read tracts against slavery. Her grandson was Germantown-born Owen Wister, the author of the novel *The Virginian*. (Courtesy of Theatre Collection, Free Library of Philadelphia.)

By 1861, as the Civil War progressed, Germantown manufacturers were busy with the war effort. Mills made cloth for soldiers' uniforms. An iron manufacturing plant at Ashmead and Wakefield Streets made bayonets. Dated June 29, 1863, this poster urged citizens to enlist.

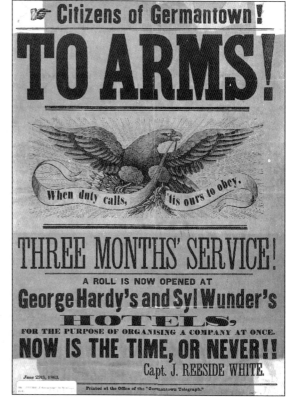

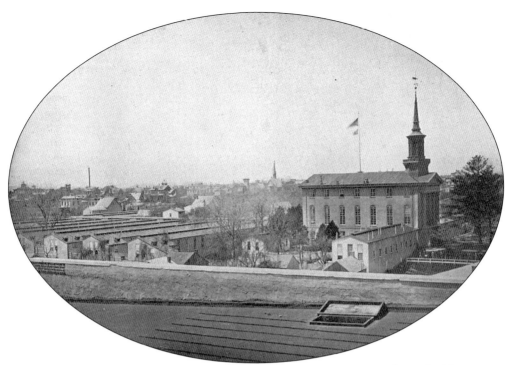

In 1862, Town Hall was offered as a military hospital. Numerous frame buildings were added, providing 630 beds. The hospital was named Cuyler, and the chief surgeon was Dr. James Darrach, later one of the founding doctors of Germantown Hospital. When Cuyler Hospital closed in 1865, the remaining patients were moved to Mower General Hospital in Chestnut Hill.

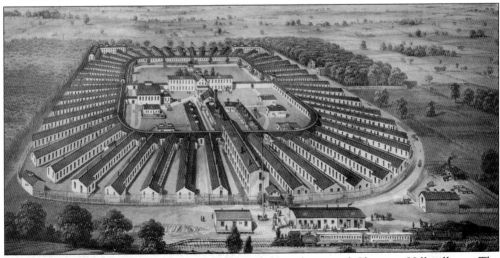

This 1863 lithograph of Mower General Hospital shows how rural Chestnut Hill still was. The hospital was designed by Philadelphia City Hall architect James McArthur Jr. on a 27-acre tract bounded by the Chestnut Hill Railroad (Wyndmoor Station, front), Abington Avenue (left), Springfield Avenue (right), and Stenton Avenue (top). It had 3,600 beds and saw 20,000 patients pass through before it closed in 1865. The bell from the chapel now hangs in Christ Ascension Lutheran Church in Chestnut Hill. (Courtesy of Chestnut Hill Historical Society.)

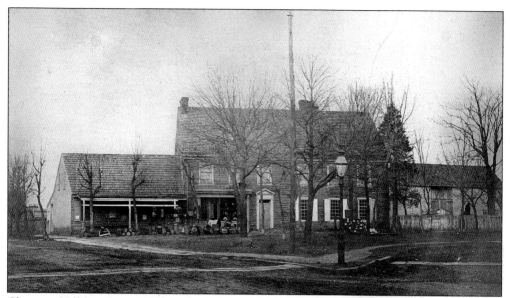

Chestnut Hill began as a settlement of farmhouses and taverns in the mid-18th century. The intersection of Germantown Avenue and Bethlehem Pike was the meeting place of two Native American trails. Yeakel's, at the fork in the road, was not one of the "great stores" which traded with the teamsters, but rather served the local population, probably bartering with farm women who came in to trade their produce for groceries and dry goods. In front of the store are barrels of oil, flour, molasses, and sugar.

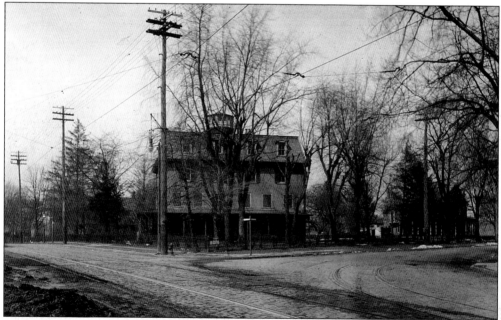

Germantown Road was muddy and icy in the winter and dusty in the summer. In 1876, the Maple Lawn Inn, also known as the Dust Pan or Miss Uhler's, was built at the fork of Germantown Avenue and Bethlehem Pike as a summer resort for Philadelphians. The new railroads brought visitors, who often decided to become permanent residents. This building was demolished in 1927.

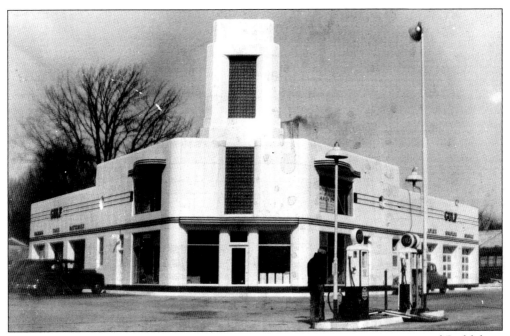

A Gulf service station succeeded the Maple Lawn Inn at Germantown Avenue and Bethlehem Pike. Shown c. 1940, this was a regional training center for service attendants. The second floor was used for classes.(Courtesy of Chestnut Hill Historical Society.)

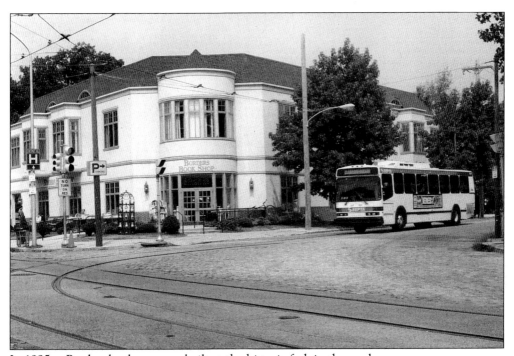

In 1995, a Borders bookstore was built at the historic fork in the road.

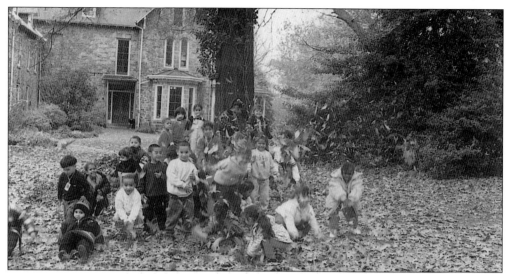

Henry Cope, a shipping merchant, bought land at Washington Lane and Chew Avenue in 1852, calling it Awbury after the English village from which the first Copes came. In 1860, he built this house for his son, Francis. The Francis Cope House is now headquarters for the Awbury Arboretum, which was established in 1916 as a public park. These preschoolers took part in a "sensory program" in the fall of 1998. The program entailed looking at bugs, mushrooms, and squirrels; touching leaves and bark; and smelling and listening to nature. (Courtesy of Awbury Arboretum.)

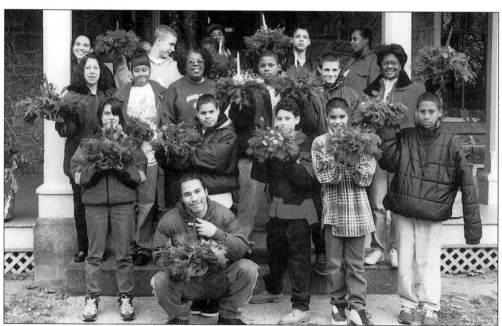

The 55-acre grounds at Awbury were designed by Germantown landscaper William Saunders. There are open meadows, a pond, woods, 200 species of trees, and farmland. These Edison High School students, working with grounds staff and AmeriCorps volunteers, took part in a yearlong project in which they planted annuals and trees, raked the grounds, and made centerpieces for their families. (Courtesy of Awbury Arboretum.)

Five

GERMANTOWN
AS A SUBURB

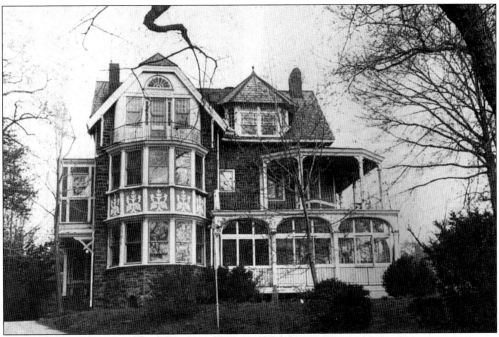

The continuing development of the railroads in the mid-19th century and the rise of a prosperous middle class led to the development of suburban villas in the Tulpehocken and Walnut Lane area. This house on Tulpehocken Street is an 1886 Queen Anne with a pyramidal slate roof, a decorative fanlight over the door, and plaster cast leaf motifs in the bay. Originally the Haines family farm, West Walnut Lane was gradually developed by architects such as Mantle Fielding, with houses in a romantic style, sometimes with castlelike features.

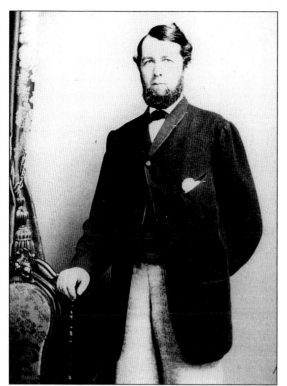

Ebenezer Maxwell (1827–1870), a cloth merchant, arrived in Philadelphia in the 1840s at the age of 21. He clerked in a dry goods firm. Then, with a partner, he began to purchase large quantities of cotton and woolen cloth from manufacturers and resell it to wholesale dealers. He was a founder of the Second Presbyterian Church at Greene and Tulpehocken Streets with other merchants, bankers, railroad executives, businessmen, and suburbanites. (Courtesy of Ebenezer Maxwell Mansion.)

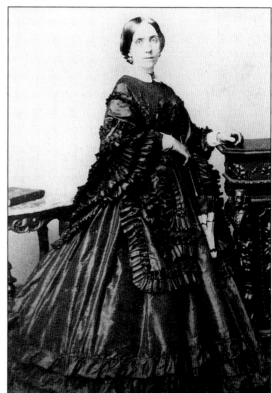

In 1853, Ebenezer Maxwell married his second cousin Anna Grizzell Smith (1831–1906), a native Philadelphian and a Quaker. They had a daughter in 1854 and moved to West Walnut Lane and then to Tulpehocken Street. (Courtesy of Ebenezer Maxwell Mansion.)

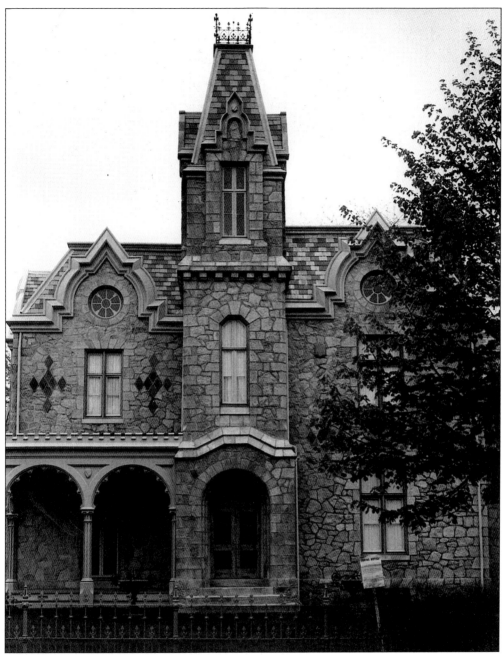

The Ebenezer Maxwell Mansion is the only restored Victorian mansion in Philadelphia that is open to the public. It was saved from demolition by a dedicated group of local residents and the Philadelphia Historical Commission. Located at Greene and Tulpehocken Streets, it was built in 1859. It is in the Gothic style and is noted for its polygonal stonework shapes, gray stone, and polychromatic slate roof. Exemplifying the tastes of the rising middle class, the house had central heat, indoor plumbing, and running water. The Maxwells lived in it for only two years. (Courtesy of Ebenezer Maxwell Mansion.)

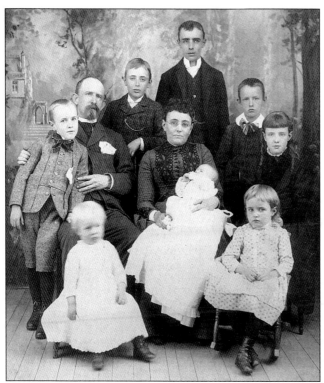

From the 1860s on, families who could afford it had their portraits taken professionally. A number of local photographers had studios in Germantown or, like Frederick Gutekunst, lived in Germantown and had a studio in downtown Philadelphia. David Hinkle (1836–1916) had a popular studio at 5405 Germantown Avenue from *c.* 1863. This 1889 photograph, by Dungan's Studio at Germantown Avenue and Mermaid Lane in Chestnut Hill, shows William and Amanda Emhardt and their children—Fred, Will, Amy, Ned, Spencer, May, Charley, and Harrison—on the couple's 16th wedding anniversary. Emhardt was president of the Germantown Mutual Fire Insurance Company.

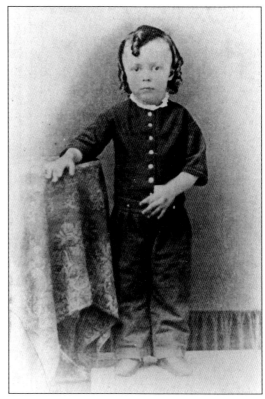

This portrait by George Lenzi is of Horace Yeakle Bates, who died February 17, 1855 at the age of 4 years and 23 days.

Elizabeth Holden Belcher (1877–1972) was often photographed by her father Alfred Holden (1852–1926), who had a studio at 5514 Germantown Avenue. This portrait was taken *c.* 1890.

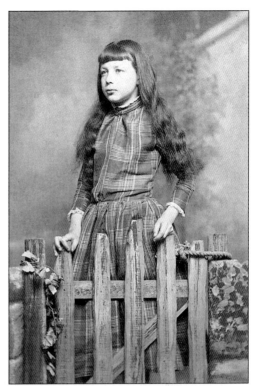

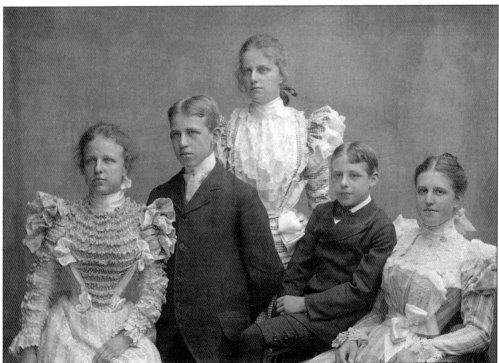

This 1895–1896 photograph shows the fashionably dressed teenage children of Pelham residents John and Mary Boltz. They are Mamie, John, Helen, Robert, and Clara.

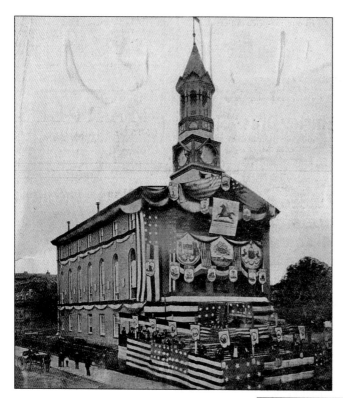

Town Hall is seen here decorated in 1877 to celebrate the 100th anniversary of the Battle of Germantown. After consolidation with Philadelphia in 1854, many had considered a town hall unnecessary since Germantown's life as a separate township was ending. For political reasons, however, this building was erected in 1855. It was designed by Napoleon LeBrun, Philadelphia's best-known architect.

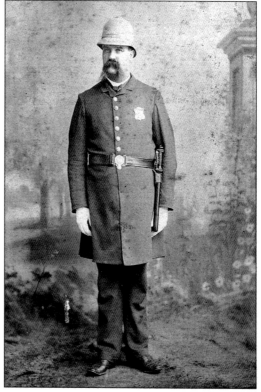

After consolidation with Philadelphia, a police station was set up in Town Hall and 12 full-time policemen were hired under the mayor's patronage. Until then, officers worked part time. The cells in the basement of Town Hall were used mostly for cases of assault and battery, intoxication, and disorderly conduct. Because of sentiment that uniforms were undemocratic, the police were not uniformed until 1858. Officer Sylvester Keyser (1843–1916) is seen here c. 1885.

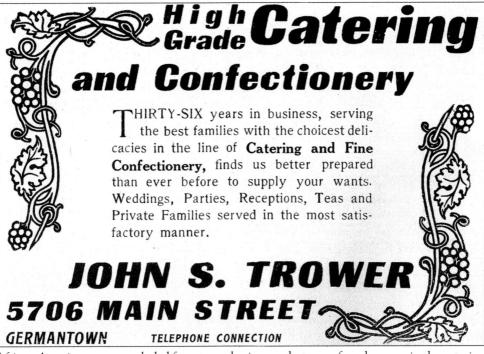

African Americans were excluded from many businesses, but some found success in the catering trade. John Sheppard Trower (1849–1911) began as an oyster opener, sold pies at railroad stations, and then opened his own business in 1870 at 5706 Germantown Avenue (now the Tropicoro Lounge). On Germantown Avenue no restaurant, even those owned by African Americans such as Trower, served black customers until 1922. Trower invested in real estate and became a local philanthropist. According to newspaper obituaries, he was "the wealthiest negro in Pennsylvania."

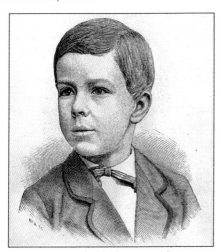 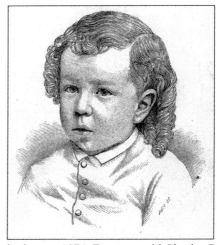

America's first recorded kidnapping for ransom took place in 1874. Four-year-old Charley Ross, right, and his brother, Walter, were abducted near their home on West Walnut Lane. Walter was released, but Charley was never seen again. According to Ella Wister Haines, "The meadows and woods were out of bounds in my childhood. The recent kidnapping of poor little Charley Ross kept all parents in a state of terror."

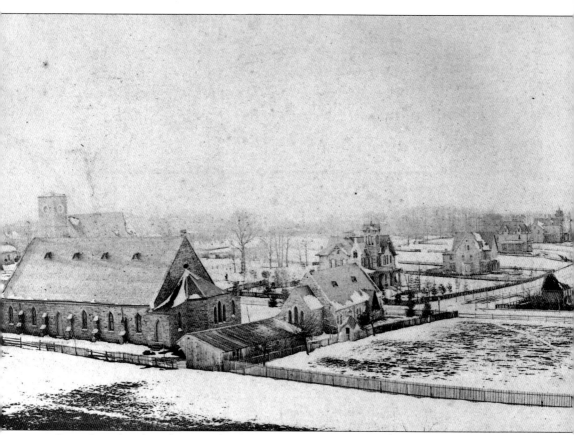

Once the railroad on the east side of Germantown was extended to Chestnut Hill in 1854, the number of wealthy Philadelphians building summer homes there increased. This photograph, taken from a rooftop on Summit Street, shows some of the first development of north Chestnut Hill. Behind the warming sheds of the old St. Paul's Episcopal Church (built in 1863–64) is the original 1856 chapel, which still stands. Behind this, at the corner of Norwood Avenue and East Chestnut Hill Avenue, is a house designed by Samuel Sloan. This house is now gone, but a twin of it can be seen at the southeast corner of Greene Street and Walnut Lane. In the back left is Our Mother of Consolation Catholic Church. The west side of Germantown and Chestnut Hill remained rural and undeveloped until the Pennsylvania Railroad opened in 1884. (Courtesy of Chestnut Hill Historical Society.)

Janes M.E. Church, seen in an 1890 photograph, was organized in 1872 as a mission of Zoar M.E. Church, the "pioneer church of African Methodism." This church, at Belfield and Haines, was used until 1898. In 1927, a new church was built at the current site, 47 East Haines Street.

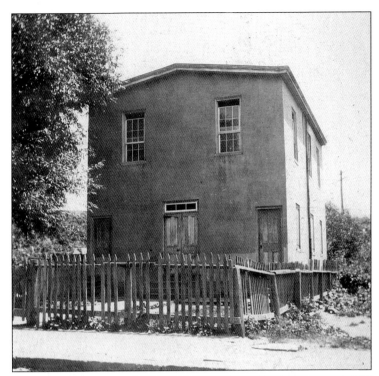

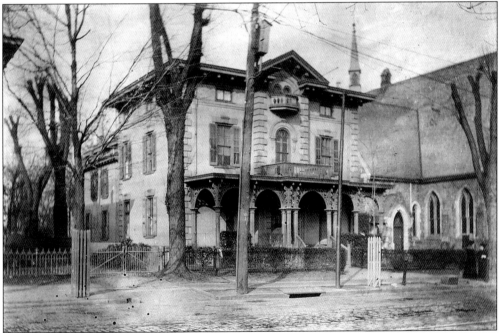

To combat the temptations of drink for working men and women, a group of Episcopal ministers formed the Workingmen's Club in 1877, offering a mix of religion and recreation. In 1883, the club moved to this building (now demolished) at 66 West Chelten Avenue next to the First Presbyterian Church in Germantown. The building included a 500-seat theater. In 1894, the club merged with the YMCA and sold the building to the church.

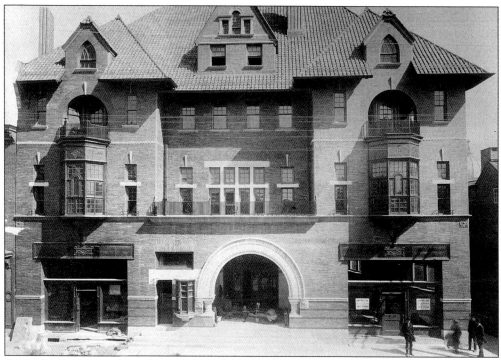

A YMCA had formed briefly in 1858 and restarted in 1871, meeting in various locations. In 1892, they erected this building on Germantown Avenue, which included a pool, gymnasium, running track, two bowling alleys, and a dormitory for 100 men—following the lead of the Workingmen's Club by providing recreation as well as religion. In 1928, the YMCA moved to its current site on Greene Street.

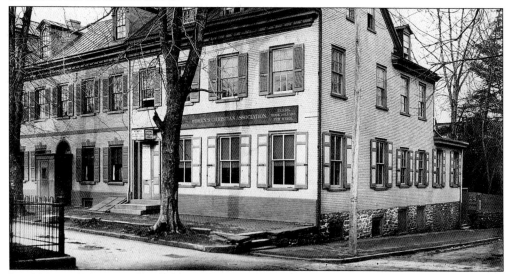

In 1870, a YWCA was founded to help young female mill workers sew, knit, read, bathe, and learn. In 1873, it moved from the cottage where Louisa May Alcott was born to the Harkness House on Market Square (shown here), now the home of the Germantown Historical Society. When the YWCA moved to a new four-story building next to Vernon Park in 1915, this house was kept for boarders (mostly young women seeking work) who were charged $3 per week.

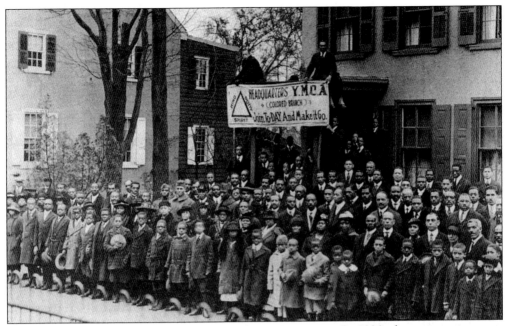

Neither the YMCA nor YWCA admitted African Americans. In 1920, the community saw a need for a new building for the "Colored YMCA," then located on West Rittenhouse Street. Through their efforts and with the help of a philanthropist, African Americans purchased a site at 132 West Rittenhouse Street for a new building. YMCAs such as this also provided lodging for visiting African Americans. (Courtesy of Mount Zion Baptist Church of Germantown.)

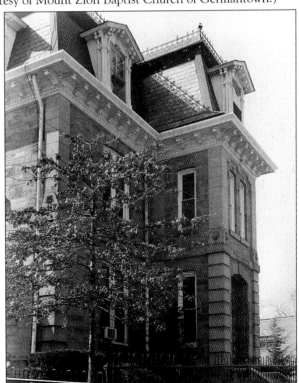

In 1918, a YWCA for African-American women was founded, using a building at 6128 Germantown Avenue (formerly the Megargee mansion, now Settlement Music School). Known as the Branch Y, it had a gymnasium and classrooms, but no pool. Girls could join the Girl Reserves, clubs within the Y that offered talks, parties, games, and crafts. In 1946, membership in the original YWCA was opened to all, and in 1952 the Branch Y closed.

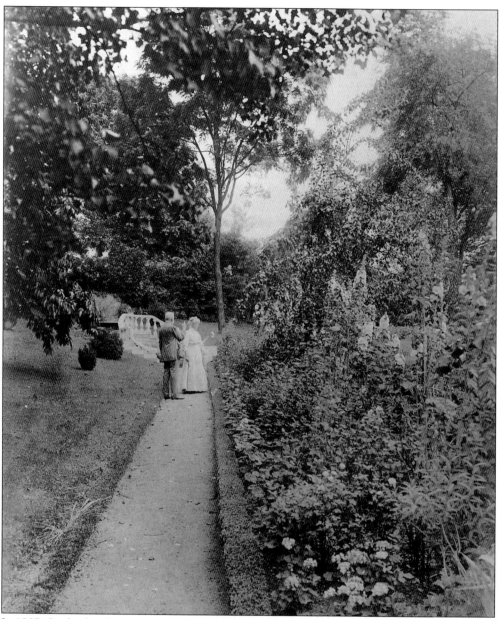

In 1887, Quaker brother and sister John and Lydia Morris began to develop their estate, Compton. Their wealth came from the I.P. Morris Company, an iron-manufacturing plant founded by their father. The Morrises traveled widely in Europe, Asia, and the United States, gathering ideas, crafts, and plants. They are seen here *c.* 1913 in the flower garden, with its boxwood edging, geraniums, phlox, and hollyhocks. This garden became a rose garden in 1924. The balustrade in the back is known as "Lydia's Seat." There are more than 10,000 labeled plants and 30 State Champion trees. The Morris Arboretum is on the National Register of Historic Places as a Victorian landscape and is noted for its historical architectural features, contemporary sculpture, and specialty gardens. In 1932, the arboretum opened to the public for recreation and research. (Courtesy of the Morris Arboretum of the University of Pennsylvania.)

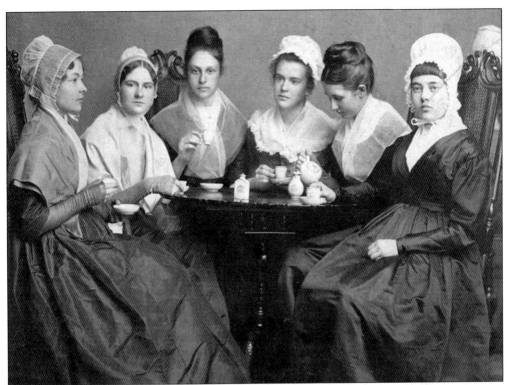

Dressed as early Quakers, these girls of the 1880 graduating class of Germantown Friends School are, from left to right, Madgie Jenkins, May Corse, Anna Cope, Anna Wharton Smith, Carrie Carter, and Lillie Bacon.

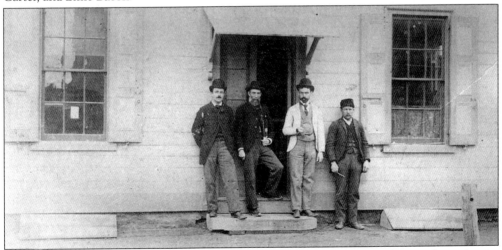

This photograph of the Mount Airy Post Office at 7153–55 Germantown Avenue (now the site of a pizza shop) was taken in 1896. Postmaster A.W. Thomas is second from left. Before it was the post office, this site was the office of Thomas's lumberyard and the first home of the Mount Airy library. Before 1816, there seems to have been no regular system for mail delivery. After that, postmasters were appointed politically, alternating between Democrats and Whigs. At the time of the photograph, there were four deliveries every day in business districts and three in residential districts.

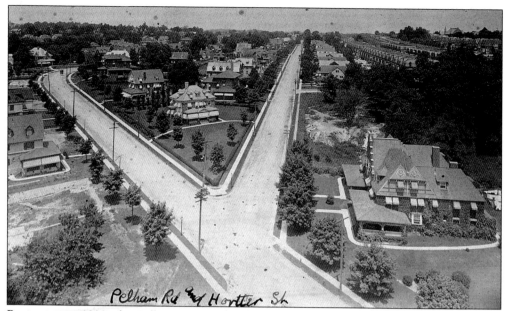

Pelham Rd & of Hortter St

Beginning in 1893, the Pelham area was developed on the estate of George W. Carpenter. Pelham's houses, designed for large families with servants, were built for the new mercantile class. Owners of Pelham houses included William Braun (Pennsylvania Lawn Mower Company), Florence Jules Heppe (Heppe Piano Company), John Dexter McIlhenny (manufacturer of gas meters), Franklin Baker (importer of coconut products), and Chester Albright (Philadelphia Toboggan Company). They tended to belong to the same clubs, such as the Germantown Cricket Club, the Union League, and the Automobile Club of Germantown, which had over 100 Pelham men in it.

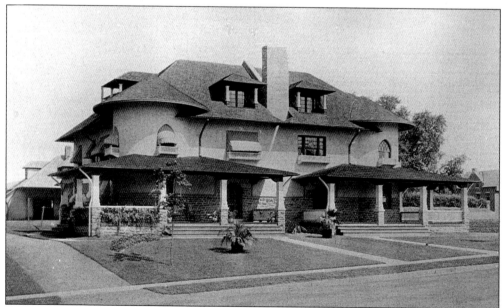

The houses in Pelham were of various architectural styles. This pair of Spanish-style round-tower houses on West Hortter Street, with roughcast plaster and dark brownish-red shingles, was designed by Charles Keen and Frank Mead.

76

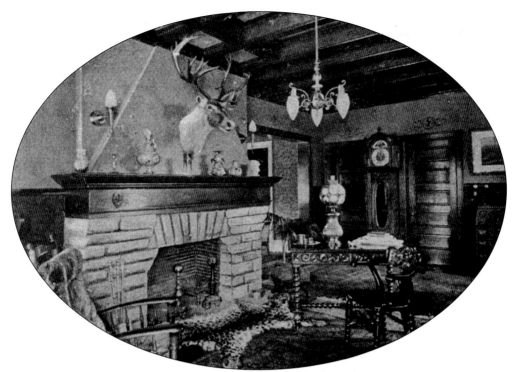

Pelham houses were hooked up to gas and electric lines and were heated by a steam plant at Pelham Road and Hortter Street. The underground pipes helped to melt ice and snow on the streets.

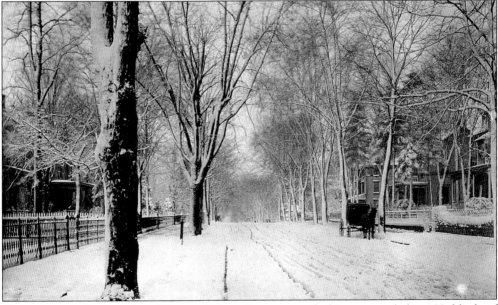

Germantown photographer Thomas Shoemaker captured this scene of the 100 block of Tulpehocken Street in winter 1891. The name Tulpehocken comes from a word meaning "land of turtles," Turtles being a clan of the Lenni Lenape. The street name was first recorded in 1850.

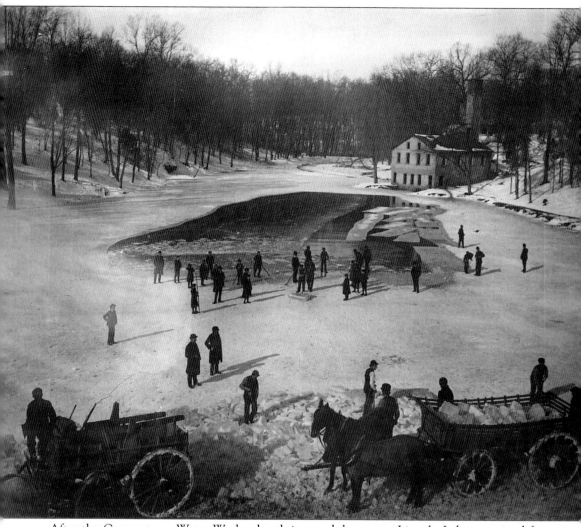

After the Germantown Water Works closed, its pond, known as Lincoln Lake, remained for years and was used for skating, ice cutting, and an occasional baptism. A catalpa-shaded lane ran from Wayne Avenue at Tulpehocken Street down to the pond. This 1884 photograph by J. Mitchell Elliot shows ice-cutting on the pond.

Charles J. Wister Jr. (1822–1910) was the last of the Wister family to live at Grumblethorpe. He was an artist, writer, musician, and amateur scientist. His father raised pigs, pressed cider, kept weather records, and built an observatory and a forge. After 1910, ownership of the house was shared by Owen Wister, the author of *The Virginian*, and Alexander Wister, although neither lived there. In the 1940s, the Philadelphia Society for Preservation of Landmarks took over the care of Grumblethorpe, and restoration to its colonial style began in 1956. It is open to the public.

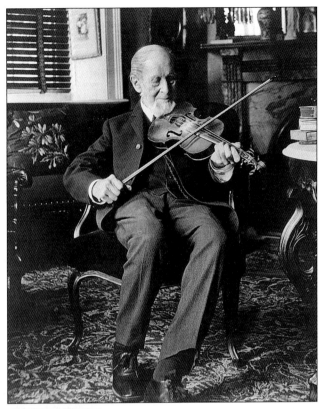

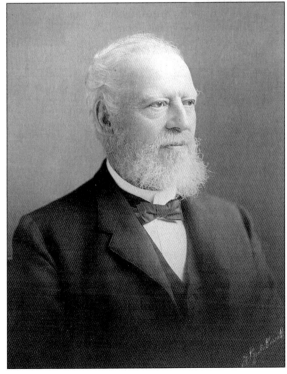

Thomas Meehan (1826–1901) was a noted nurseryman, botanist, and editor. He worked at Bartram's Garden after emigrating from England, and then started his own nursery at Germantown Avenue and what is now Meehan Street. He sold plants all over the world. In 1870, he bought land at Chew and Phil-Ellena Streets, and his nurseries eventually covered 75 acres. He became a city councilman and was a strong advocate for city parks.

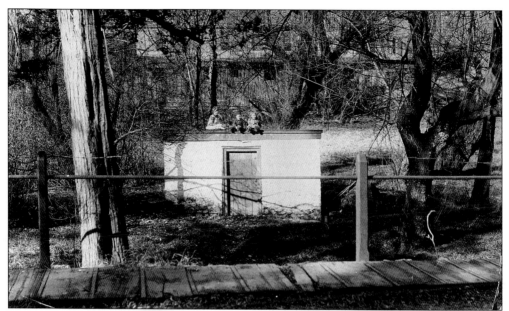

John Christopher Meng, who made cider and vinegar, lived in a house where Vernon House now stands. During the Battle of Germantown, the British used his house as a hospital (vinegar was an antiseptic). This springhouse, with Meng's descendants sitting on its roof, could still be seen in Meng's Meadow in 1881.

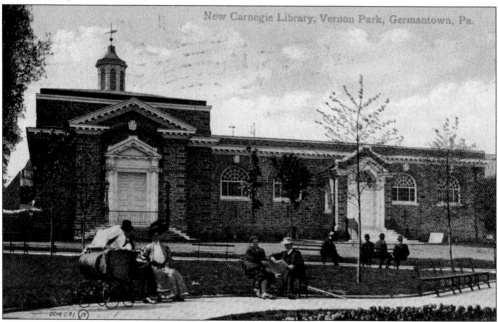

As a member of the Philadelphia city council, Thomas Meehan played a vital role in saving Meng's old property and its trees. The city bought the property in 1892 and created Vernon Park. A gift from Andrew Carnegie enabled the city to build this public library in Vernon Park in 1907. Since 1986, the library building has been home to Center in the Park, which focuses primarily on the needs of older people. Vernon House is now home to Friends of Vernon Park and the Central Germantown Council.

Six

FROM SUBURB TO CITY

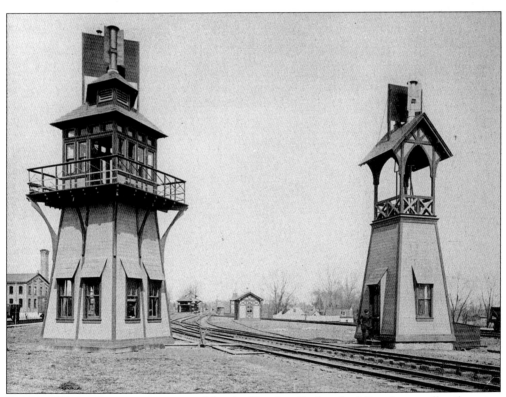

In 1881, Wayne Junction was opened by the Reading Railroad, although a small rail station had been at that location since 1857. These Victorian signal towers were built to control the junction, which became one of the central freight and passenger depots in the region. Major industries, notably Midvale Steel, opened near the station. At the same time, the large estates of Germantown were being broken up and sold to developers who built housing for employees of the new factories.

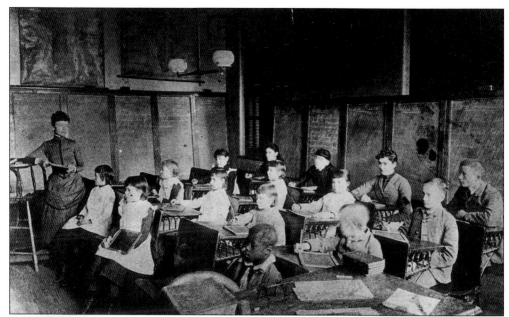

Founded in 1820, the Pennsylvania School for the Deaf moved to Mount Airy in 1892. This photograph shows a typical class of upper-school students in the late 1890s. Since 1984, the Pennsylvania School for the Deaf has occupied the former Germantown Academy site at Greene Street and School House Lane. Their old site now belongs to New Covenant Church. (Courtesy of Pennsylvania School for the Deaf.)

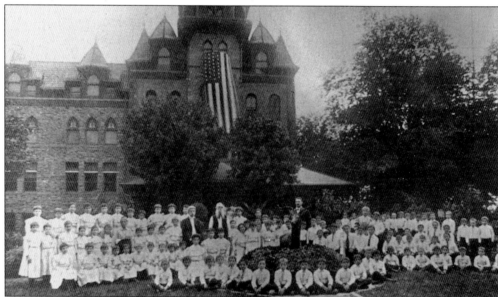

Children who were orphaned faced a bleak future in the late 19th century. Many worked for a pittance in the mills, lived in hovels, or ran in the streets. The Jewish Foster Home was set up so that indigent Jewish children might "be rescued from the evils of ignorance and vice, comfortably provided for, and instructed in moral and religious duties." In 1881, the home moved from downtown Philadelphia to Church Lane near Chew Avenue for its wholesome, rural atmosphere. It was dedicated in 1892.

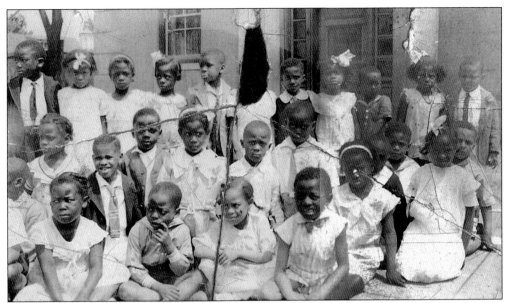

The Joseph E. Hill School on West Rittenhouse Street was founded in 1868 by William Cole and renamed for Hill, a pioneer African-American educator in Philadelphia. The first school for black students in Germantown, it had a female principal, Marie E. Roland, and six African-American women as teachers. Although black students had the legal right to attend any public school after 1881, only a few actually attended white schools. Seen here is a 1933 class.

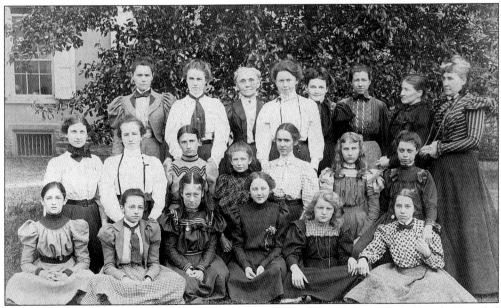

The Stevens School was a private school for girls that emphasized the study of French. Founded in 1869, it was on West Walnut Lane, where this class of 1901–1902 is shown. In the 1930s, the school offered courses for high school graduates, brides-to-be, and young matrons "who are interested in establishing ideal, satisfying homes and in administering them efficiently and scientifically."

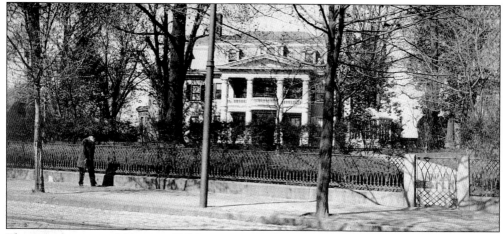

The Germantown and Chestnut Hill Improvement Association pushed for a new high school for Germantown in the first decade of the 20th century. The board of education bought the Edgar H. Butler estate, seen here, and adjoining grounds south of High Street, accepting the proviso that the trees would be preserved after the school was built. Besides Germantown High School, 11 other new schools were built in this period to accommodate an increase in population.

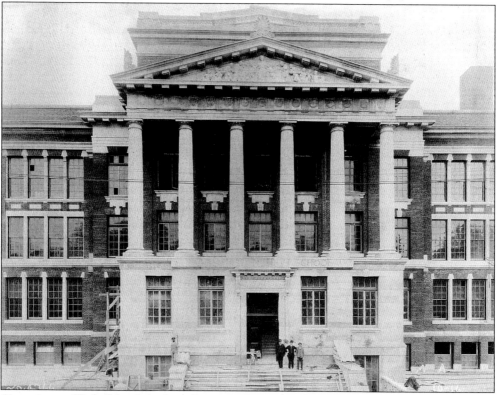

Germantown High School, built in Georgian Revival style, is shown here before the pouring of the front steps in 1915. Boys and girls were taught separately at the new school; in fact, they were physically separated by iron gates. The first class of boys and girls graduated in 1917. The school was open to African Americans from the beginning but very few attended at first. There are currently 1,600 students.

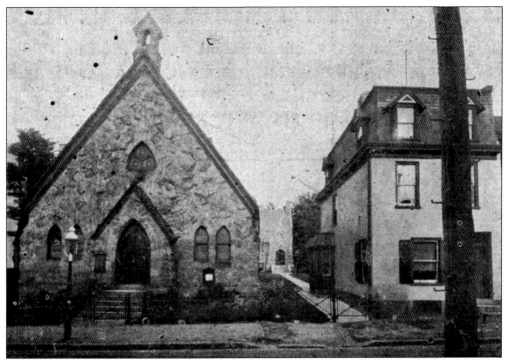

St. Barnabas Episcopal Church was organized in 1904 by a group of white Episcopalians led by Dr. Samuel Upjohn, rector of St. Luke's Episcopal Church. This group's members, who had served together at the Industrial Home for Colored Women on Armat Street, started St. Barnabas as a mission church for African Americans. They bought the unoccupied building adjacent to the Hill Public School at Rittenhouse and McCallum Streets for the church. In 1968, the mission church closed, and St. Luke's and St. Barnabas became one.

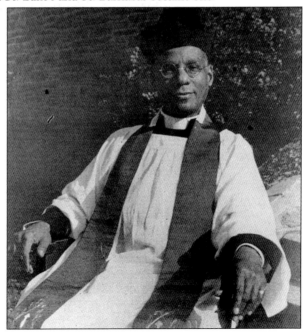

In 1907, Rev. E. Sydnor Thomas became pastor of St. Barnabas and served for almost 50 years. He managed to obtain an organ for the church by raising half of the cost, with the rest matched by philanthropist Andrew Carnegie.

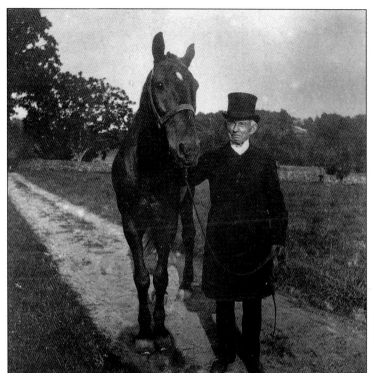

Dr. William Rush Dunton's coachman, who drove him to appointments, is seen here *c.* 1900. Dunton was a surgeon at Cuyler Hospital during the Civil War and stayed in Germantown. He saw patients in his office in the morning and then visited others by horse and carriage in the afternoons.

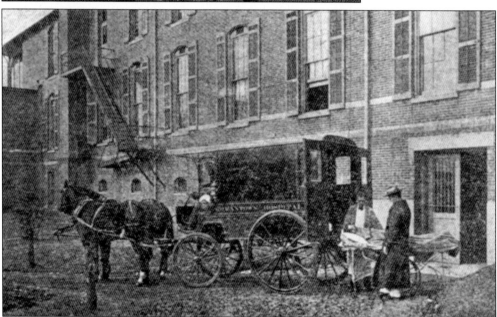

Germantown Hospital started in 1870 as a successor to Cuyler Hospital and the Germantown Dispensary. Known as the "Three D's," Doctors Dunton, James Darrach, and Robert Downs had their own practices but also provided free care at the hospital. They treated industrial accidents at the mills, quarries, and railroads as well as the usual ailments. A Board of Lady Visitors raised money, inspected the hospital for cleanliness, and sewed huge quantities of linens, towels, and gowns. One of the hospital's horse-drawn ambulances is shown here in 1904.

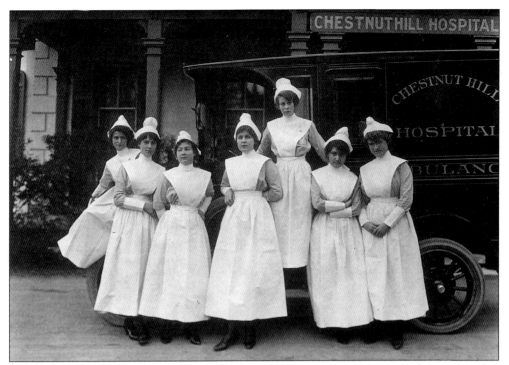

This group of Chestnut Hill Hospital nurses is seen probably in spring 1917. One of them married a doctor from the hospital and had to drop out of nursing school before graduation, as married nurses were not permitted. After its humble beginnings in 1904 on Gravers Lane, the hospital acquired the Norrington mansion at 8815 Germantown Avenue and began its expansion. (Courtesy of Chestnut Hill Historical Society.)

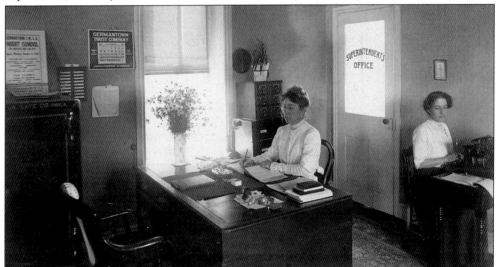

The Germantown Relief Society began in 1873 during a business depression in Germantown, which especially hurt mill workers. Its volunteers saw it as their mission to help poor families to make permanent changes in their situation. They wanted to help the worthy and discourage professional beggars and indolents. They never gave money, only food, clothing, and fuel. Its offices, shown here in 1913, were at 21 West Harvey Street.

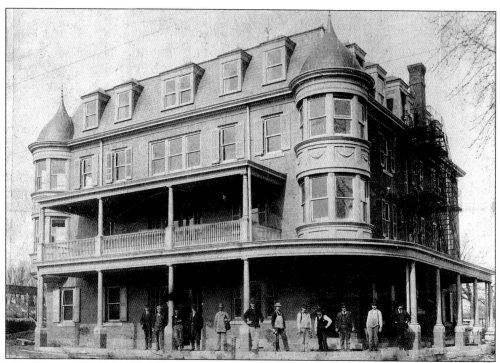

The Chestnut Hill Hotel, at 8229 Germantown Avenue, is seen at its completion in 1894. The contractor was probably Jacob Uhle. The hotel was renovated in 1957–1958 along colonial lines.(Courtesy of Chestnut Hill Historical Society.)

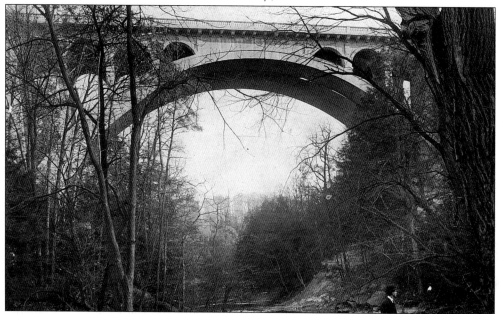

The Walnut Lane Bridge over the Wissahickon ravine was completed in 1908. Before that time, the only way from Germantown to Roxborough was long, indirect, and steeply graded. The bridge was the longest concrete span then in existence, and its engineering attracted wide interest. The span is 585 feet long and the center is 133 feet above the creek.

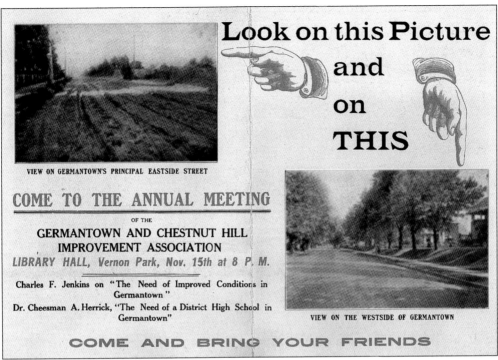

Look on this Picture and on **THIS**

VIEW ON GERMANTOWN'S PRINCIPAL EASTSIDE STREET

COME TO THE ANNUAL MEETING

OF THE

GERMANTOWN AND CHESTNUT HILL IMPROVEMENT ASSOCIATION

LIBRARY HALL, Vernon Park, Nov. 15th at 8 P. M.

Charles F. Jenkins on "The Need of Improved Conditions in Germantown"

Dr. Cheesman A. Herrick, "The Need of a District High School in Germantown"

VIEW ON THE WESTSIDE OF GERMANTOWN

COME AND BRING YOUR FRIENDS

The Germantown and Chestnut Hill Improvement Association, a men's organization, was formed in 1906 and was followed by many other new civic associations. The association employed Jacob Bockius to investigate and remedy complaints, a position he held until 1932. On this c. 1910 poster, the association's concerns were road improvements and a new high school for Germantown (Germantown High School was opened in 1915). There were committees devoted to education, police, fire, steam and street railways, park and playgrounds, zoning, and parking. The association also organized outings for its members.

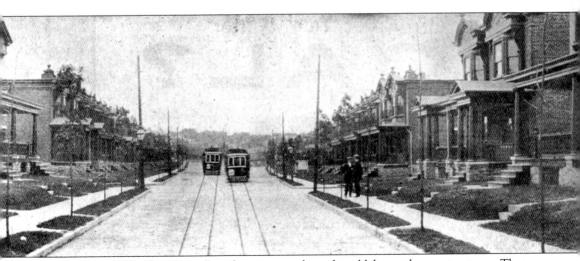

Beginning c. 1895, electric trolleys began to replace the old horse-drawn streetcars. These trolleys are seen at Twentieth and East Chelten Avenue.

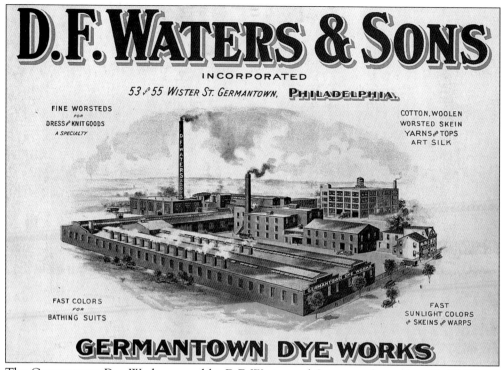

The Germantown Dye Works, owned by D.F. Waters and Sons, was located at 53–55 Wister Street at the turn of the 20th century. An interesting aspect of the Germantown dyeing industry is its influence on Navajo weavings. From c. 1863 to 1910, huge quantities of yarn— which were brightly colored with the new imported aniline dyes, especially reds—made their way west where they were woven by the Navajo, at first during their internment by the U.S. government. Eventually these eye-dazzling weavings fell out of favor as customers preferred the traditional Navajo dyes, but they are now popular collectibles.

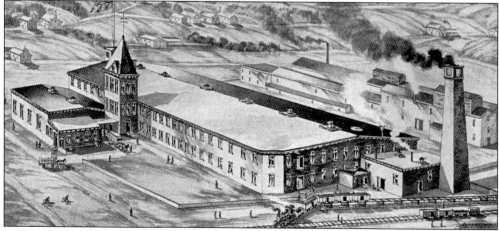

Mills such as the Germantown Spinning Mill, seen here in 1899, continued to employ many workers. But when Conyers Button, the son of the founder of Germantown Hosiery Mills, decided that he had acquired sufficient wealth, he closed his plant and sold the land for housing development. Other mills, including Wakefield Mills, also closed around the turn of the century.

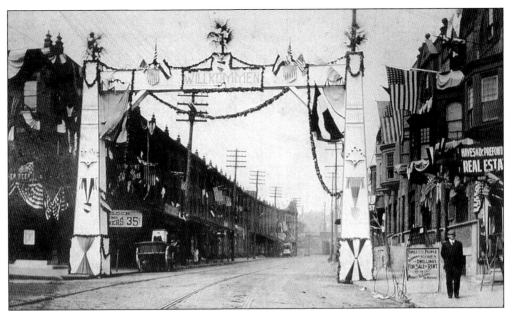

"Wilkommen 1683–1908" says the Arch of Welcome raised at Roberts and Germantown Avenues, the entry to Germantown. The arch marked the 225th anniversary of Germantown's founding. The central celebration was the laying of a cornerstone in Vernon Park for a sculpture commemorating the founders of Germantown. That design was abandoned, and a new sculptor designed the statue now in the park. (Courtesy of Robert M. Skaler collection).

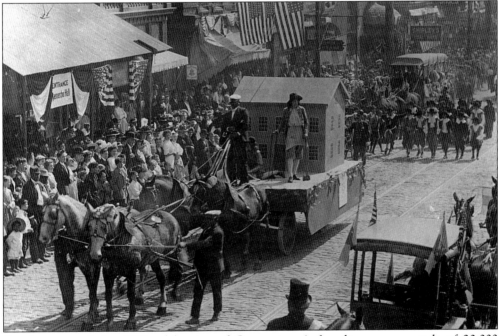

Another part of the 1908 celebration of Germantown's founding was a parade of 20,000 people, representing Native Americans, German settlers, Wissahickon hermits, Continental soldiers, George Washington, and Gilbert Stuart. Nearly 3,000 school children were treated to sandwiches, ice cream, and coffee at Town Hall.

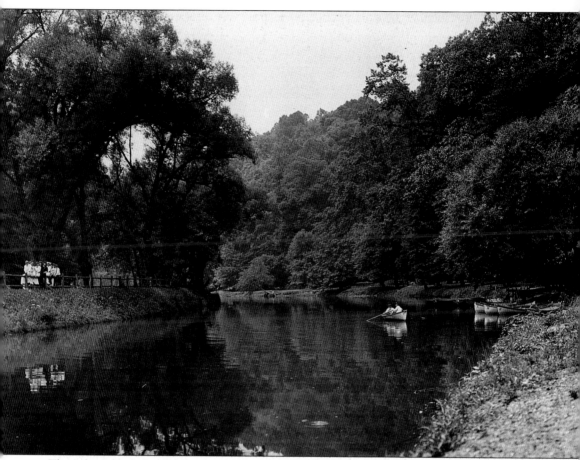

This photograph by Philip H. Moore (1879–1958) shows boating and sightseeing on the Wissahickon Creek in the early 20th century. The Wissahickon continues to be a place of recreation as it has been for three centuries. Efforts by many local residents to keep automobiles out of the park were successful. In 1964, the Wissahickon Valley was designated a National Natural Landmark.

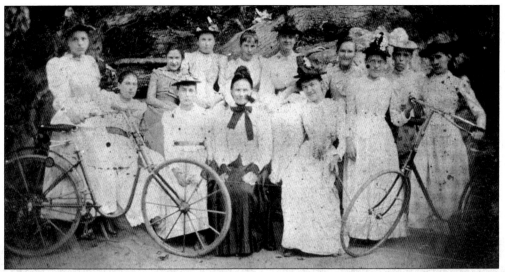

Edith Jelden and her friends from Sunday school enjoy a picnic outing in the Wissahickon in 1885. Jelden (second from the left) was the daughter of Rev. Frederick Jelden of St. Thomas Lutheran Church at Herman and Morton Streets. After St. Michael's Church switched to English services, Lutherans who preferred German-language services founded St. Thomas' in 1860. Edith Jelden later became a probation officer and president of the Women's Germantown Republican Club. She died where she was raised at 6204 Morton Street.

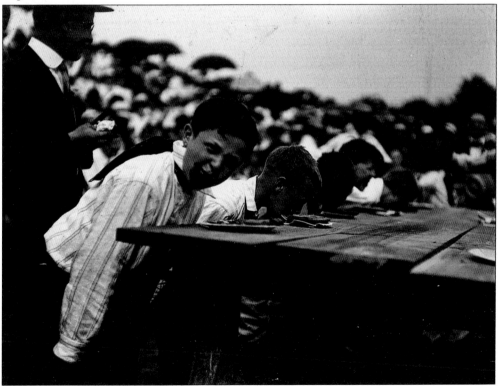

Among entertainment at the beginning of the 20th century was this pie-eating contest in Chestnut Hill *c.* 1905.

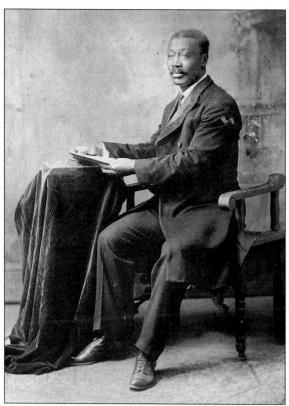

In 1871, a parcel of land on West Rittenhouse Street was purchased for a new church and in 1890 Rev. Morton Winston, a former slave, became pastor of Mount Zion Baptist Church. The church building at 41 West Rittenhouse Street was completed in 1896. At the time of Winston's death in 1928, Mount Zion was the largest Protestant congregation in Germantown, with more than 4,000 members. (Courtesy of Mount Zion Baptist Church of Germantown).

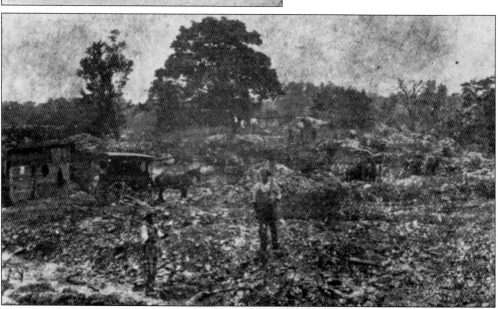

The stone for the building was donated by William Byrd, an African-American contractor and realtor who owned a quarry and was superintendent of Mount Zion's Sunday school. His quarry furnished stone for many of the Pelham houses. Rev. Morton Winston, formerly a stone cutter, helped to build the church himself. Caterer John Trower helped underwrite the building and donated a stained glass window.

George W. Deane's office on Germantown Avenue is seen here. Deane was an African-American realtor who owned a good deal of property in Germantown. He rented it to African Americans who came from the South as jobs opened up during WWI. As was customary until the 1940s, he did not attempt to introduce blacks into all-white neighborhoods. Several neighborhoods, such as Pulaskitown (Coulter to Hansberry, Wayne to Morris) and the area near Morton and Haines Streets, were already mixed. Deane married the daughter of Rev. Morton Winston, the pastor of Mount Zion Baptist Church.

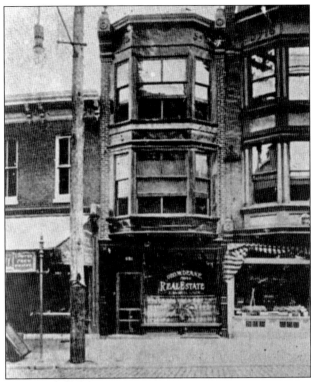

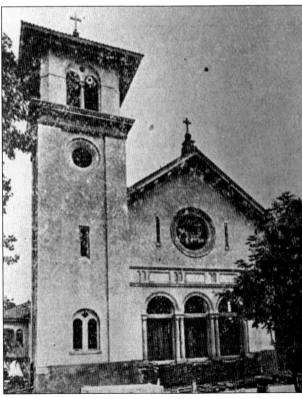

St. Catherine of Siena, a Roman Catholic Church, was built in 1914 on West Penn Street as an offshoot of St. Vincent de Paul Catholic Church for African Americans. It was funded in part by Mother Katherine Drexel and built in the style of the Spanish missions in California with a red tile roof. It was the center for African-American Catholics in the area until it closed in 1993. It is now the Church of the Lord Jesus Christ of the Apostolic Faith.

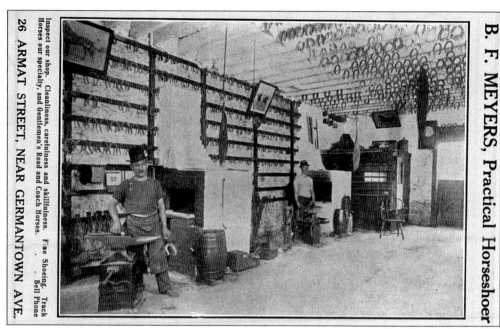

Horses and carriages continued to be used into the 20th century, despite the advent of the automobile. This 1909 advertisement is for B.F. Meyers, Practical Horseshoer, at 26 Armat Street. The ad notes, "Track horses our specialty, and Gentlemen's Road and Coach Horses."

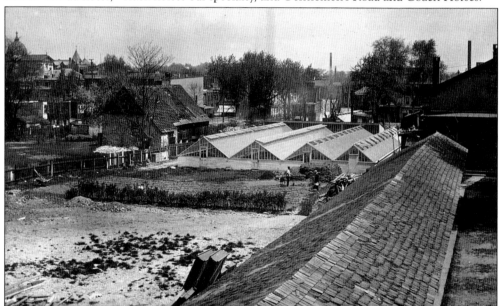

Germantown has a tradition of gardeners and nurserymen. Christian Lehman opened Germantown's first nursery before the Revolutionary War. In the 1830s, Martin Baumann had a large nursery near Manheim Street and Pulaski Avenue. His son, Louis Clapier Baumann, had greenhouses at the northeast corner of Wayne and Manheim. Other nurseries were those of Henry Woltemate on Germantown Avenue at Queen Lane, Frederick Knapp in Chestnut Hill, and Charles Miller in Mount Airy. This 1911 photograph shows a stable and greenhouses at Germantown Avenue and Maplewood Avenue.

An ad from a 1909 publication promotes McKinney's Tea and Coffee House, founded in 1898. In c. 1912, a Germantown woman recalled, "At the northeast corner of Armat [and Germantown Avenue] was McKinney's tea and coffee house. One entered, in warm weather, through a doorway protected by a lovely rustling bead portiere to the most heavenly smells—great bags of freshly roasted coffee just ready for the grinder and you could select your own combination of teas—my Mother's choice was always imperial Green and Uncolored Japan."

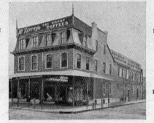

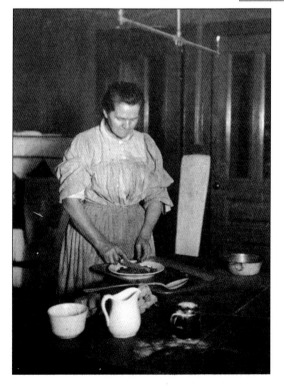

The cook of the Kingston household at Chelten Avenue and Greene Street is seen in this 1890s photograph. Domestic work and factory jobs were common employment for working-class women. Gas lighting, seen here, was introduced in Germantown in 1853 and was still in use into the 20th century. Electricity became commonly used in households in the 1890s.

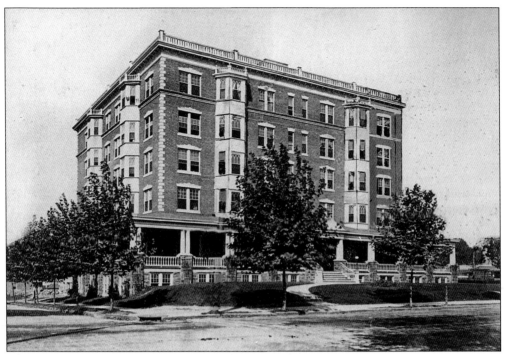

The Del Mar apartment house at the northeast corner of Chelten and Morris was built in 1903 by John DeLong. It was the first of 100 apartment buildings erected in a 24-year period to serve the expanding population. There was a rapid buildup of new housing, commerce, and factories during this period. As open space became less available, people moved to more distant suburbs.

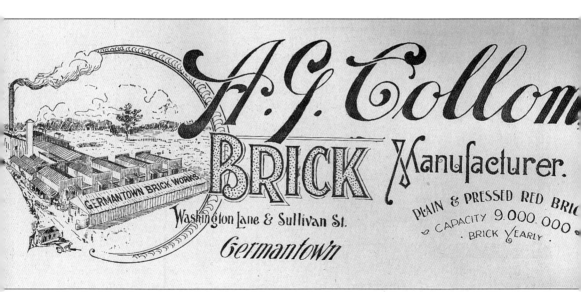

The building boom provided a lot of business for brick manufacturers. A.G. Collom's brick works at Washington Lane and Sullivan (now Ardleigh) Street is shown here in 1908. The company boasted a capacity of 9 million bricks yearly.

The extensive Justus Strawbridge estate was on Wissahickon Avenue (then called Township Line), where the Alden Park apartments were later built. The estate had greenhouses with tropical plants, model pig pens, and cow barns. According to the caption of this *c.* 1897 photograph, "A coach and four were kept here, under the care of Sam, the colored coachman, who sounded the horn on occasion of cricket match at Manheim or horse show at St. Martin's."

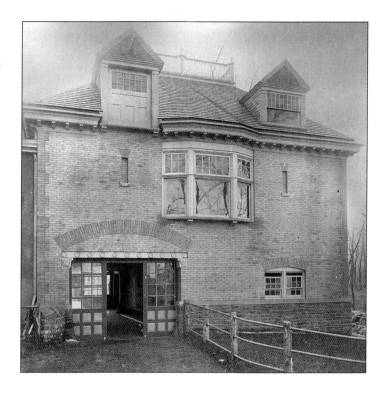

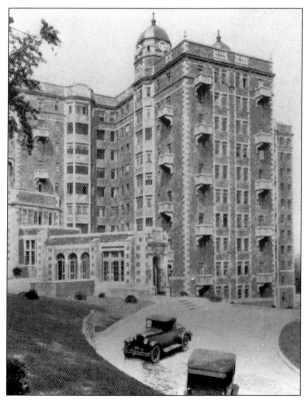

A castlelike collection of apartment buildings on a 38-acre site, Alden Park is the largest residential property on the National Register of Historic Places. The Manor was built in 1925–1926, the Kenilworth in 1927–1928, and the Cambridge in 1929. It is in Jacobean Revival style and features light red bricks, salmon-pink concrete, turrets, and balconies. (Courtesy of Alden Park.)

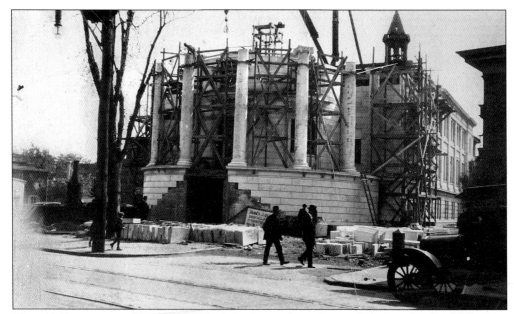

The old Germantown Town Hall, which had served as a hospital during the Civil War, was declared unsound in 1920. This new one was built at the urging of the Germantown and Chestnut Hill Improvement Association. It was dedicated on Armistice Day 1925 and contains memorial tablets to 123 Germantown soldiers who died in WWI.

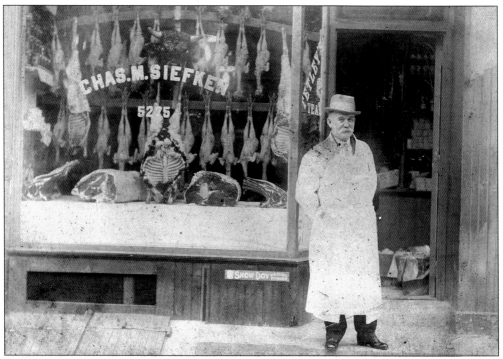

Siefken Meats was at 5275 Germantown Avenue, just below Penn Street, in the late 19th and early 20th century.

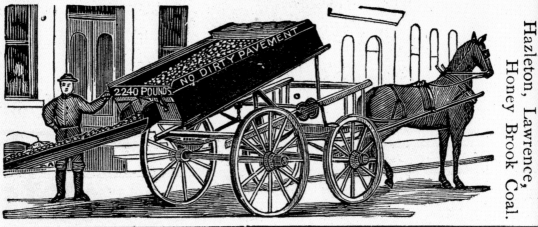

This 1884 advertisement for Charles Weiss's coal company boasts that it uses chute wagons to deliver coal across pavements or lawns and bags where necessary. "No dirt marks are left to inform the passer-by that coal has been put in the house," it reads. "What an eyesore it is to have one's property marked up by the coal dealer."

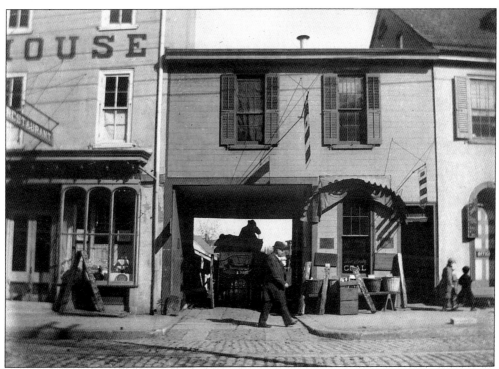

Like the inns of old, the coal yard of George E. Weiss, successor to Charles Weiss, has a drive-in entrance and courtyard, c. 1910. It was located at 5717 Germantown Avenue opposite Vernon Park. When the business began in 1846, coal cars had to be hauled from Nicetown by horses and were then returned by gravity; by 1896, locomotives hauled the coal.

101

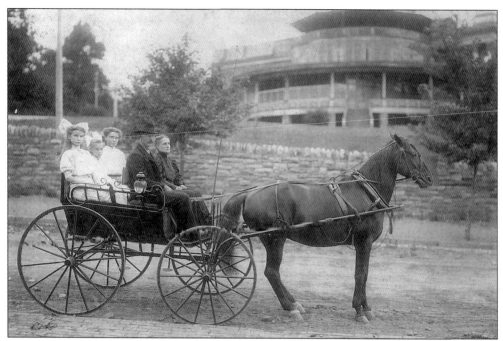

Eugene and Mary Everman, their daughters Sarah, Olive, and Addie, and Bird, the horse, take a drive in c. 1905. Eugene, a carpenter, lived at 6040 Wissahickon Avenue, which was described in city directories as part of Blue Bell Hill. (Courtesy of Dorothy Steele.)

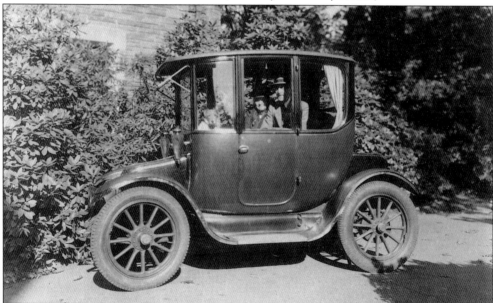

In the first decades of the 20th century, developer Dr. George Woodward owned two electric cars—a five-passenger phaeton, and this two-seater, which he guided with a tiller instead of a steering wheel. He and his wife, Gertrude, are seen here with their dog Mozart in front of their Chestnut Hill home, Krisheim. During WWII, he brought the car out of storage because of gas rationing. Drivers of horses competed with cars in the early years, but new laws required cars to stop when approaching horses. (Courtesy of Chestnut Hill Historical Society.)

Seven

NEIGHBORHOOD WITHIN A CITY

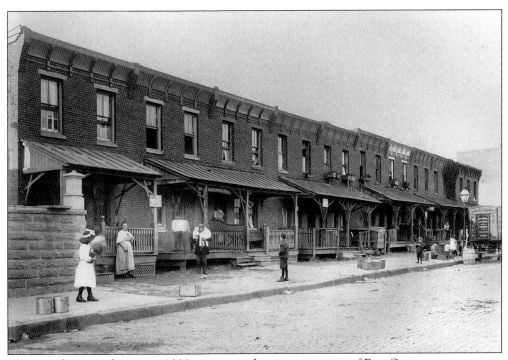

These workers' row houses, c. 1900, are situated in a poor section of East Germantown.

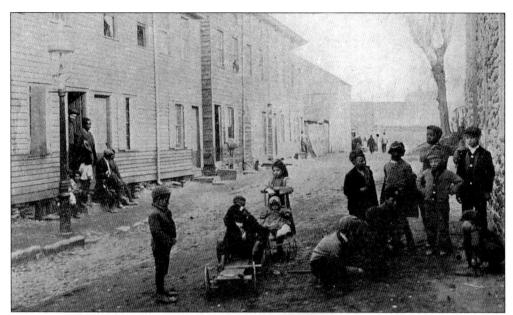

The Morton Boys Club opened in 1911 at 502–4 East Haines Street. The annual report describes this photograph as "Our immediate neighborhood in what is known as Haines Street Hollow, one of the worst sections of Germantown. Within half a mile of the building there are over 20 saloons." The club offered carpentry, cobbling, cooking, printing, and gardening, as well as sewing for girls.

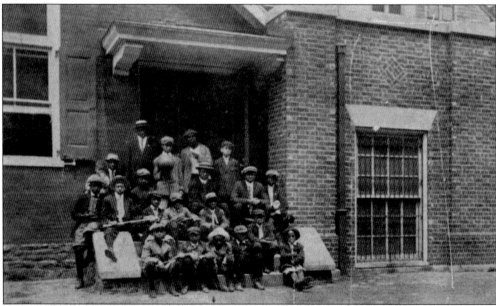

The Wissahickon Boys (or School) Club was founded in 1885 at the northeast corner of Coulter Street and Pulaski Avenue. It was organized by a group of white Quakers, led by John T. Emlen, for African-American boys. The aim was to provide wholesome activities for boys. "Boys usually get into trouble between the hours of 4 and 10 o'clock at night," notes a report. This 1912 photograph was taken in front of the club. Still active, the club meets near the original building and is open to both boys and girls.

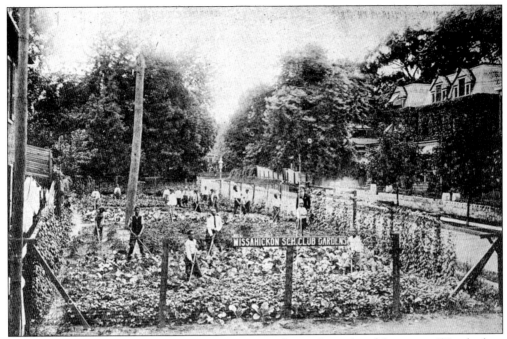

"What we are aiming at is strong, righteous, true-hearted manhood," states a Wissahickon School Club report. The club offered sports, including long-distance running; trades like upholstery, shoe repair, and basketry; and debates. Another activity was gardening, which is pictured here in 1912. In the 1950s, the young Wilt Chamberlain, Bill Cosby, and John Chaney played sports at the club, and there were dances, movies, and rollerskating.

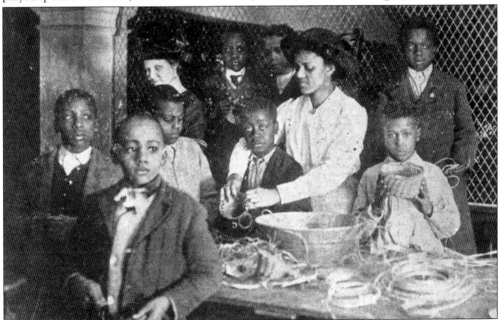

Olivia Yancey Taylor, shown here c. 1913 working with boys at the Wissahickon School Club, was a teacher and a member of Faith Presbyterian Church. She taught at the Hill School and became chair of the Negro (or Branch) YWCA.

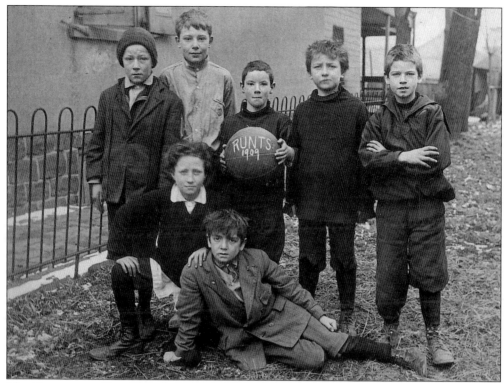

The Germantown Boys Club (for whites only) was founded in 1887 as the Boys Parlors. Its goal was the improvement of 9- to 14-year-old boys "of the poorer classes," and to shield them from "the fierce and alluring temptations of the street" by offering games, reading, and education. The club moved to various locations before settling on West Penn Street in 1898. It opened for girls in 1914. This photograph shows the 1909 Runts basketball team at the club.

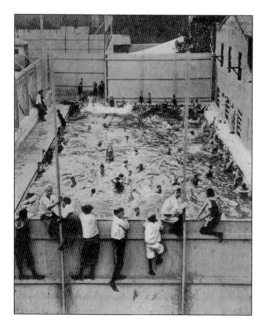

In 1905, the club became the Germantown Boys Club and in 1909 moved into a new building, still on West Penn Street. In 1911, a pool next to the building was opened and was enjoyed by many generations of boys. At the time of this picture in 1912, the pool was used by about 500 boys daily. The club, now open to both boys and girls, is still active.

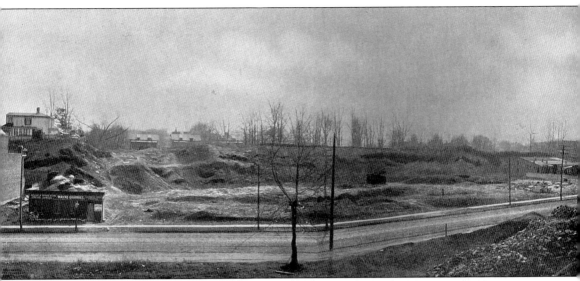

This is the site of Happy Hollow playground at Wayne Avenue opposite Logan Street c. 1910, before work began on transforming the old quarry into a recreation site. On both sides of Wayne Avenue were hills of solid rock, with few houses. After a boy drowned in the quarry, its owner, Edward W. Clark, decided to turn it into a playground. His heirs donated the 4-acre tract for Happy Hollow and another at School House Lane and Wissahickon, now known as Clark Park.

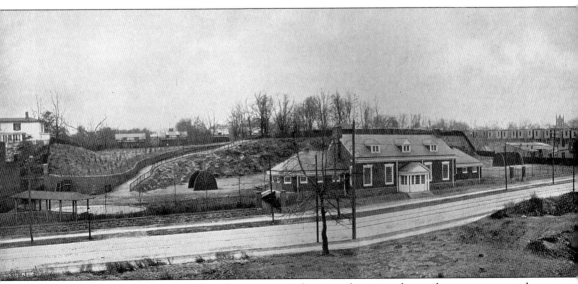

The rugged quarry was softened with terraces and grassy slopes, and a pathway was created leading up to tennis courts and clubhouse. The recreation center opened in 1911 and is active to this day. The path seen here still offers an interesting view of the old quarry site and a high point between Wayne Avenue and Pulaski Avenue. Calvary Episcopal Church can be seen at the top right.

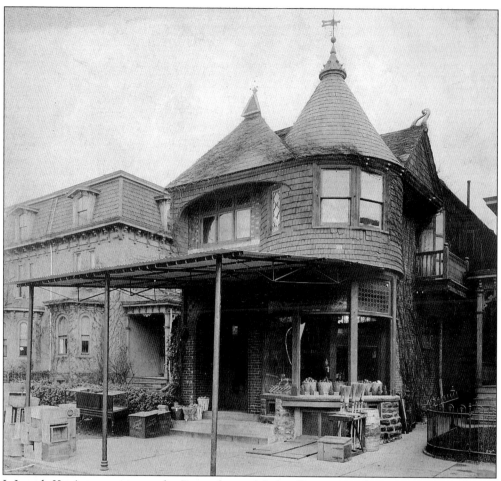

J. Joseph Katz's grocery store, the Pennsylvania Market House, seen here in 1907, was at 308 West Chelten Avenue. In the first half of the 20th century, Germantown's business district became prominent regionally, combining as it did large and small stores, excellent public transportation, locally controlled banks, and a wide range of housing and jobs.

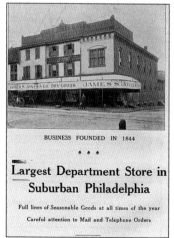

James S. Jones's general store opened in 1844, later specializing in dry goods. Known as "Lower" Jones (there was an "Upper" Jones farther up Germantown Avenue), by 1909 its advertisements claimed it was the "largest department store in suburban Philadelphia." In the early 20th century, Jones sometimes brought in eggs from his farm to sell. "Jimmy" Jones sold fabrics at Germantown and Coulter until 1978, when the store became Gaffney Fabrics.

Started in 1809, Robert Cherry's store successfully made the transition from shoe manufacturer to shoe store. As the bench-made shoe business disappeared after the Civil War, Cherry's became a retail store and repair shop. It expanded in 1904 to new buildings at 5541–7 Germantown Avenue and became the best place for men's clothing and shoes. It remained in Germantown until 1961.

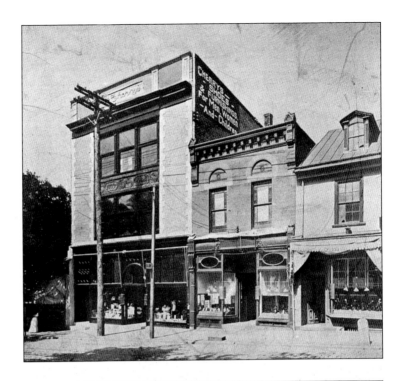

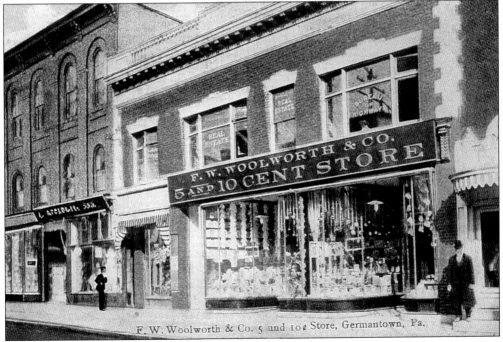

F.W. Woolworth opened on the east side of Germantown Avenue below Chelten Avenue c. 1910 (now the site of Murry's Meats). As a general store, it offered many kinds of merchandise and was the successor to stores such as Tarr's dry goods store and Miss Griffin's millinery store. It was one of the early chain stores, using mass production and mass-marketing techniques. (Courtesy of Robert M. Skaler collection).

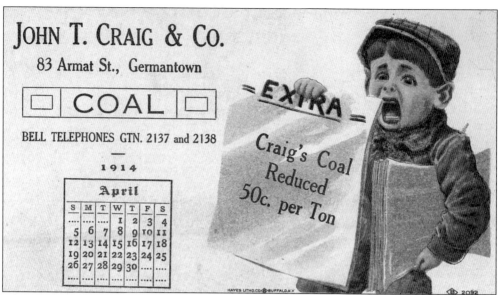

John T. Craig and Co., a coal company, started in 1898 on Armat Street. Now an oil company, it is still in business at 5800 Musgrave Street. This calendar is from 1914.

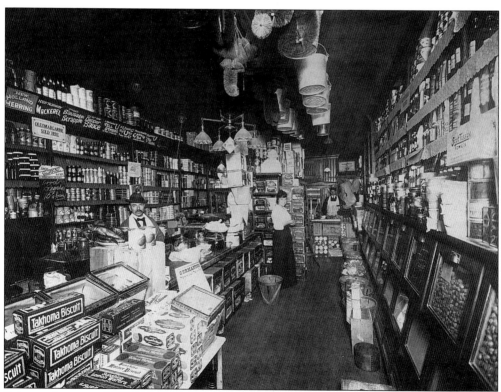

Schramm's store at 337 West Queen Lane is seen here *c.* 1900. Owned by J. Christian Schramm and John J. Schramm Jr., the store was in business until 1964. Among the items on the shelves are crackers, herring, mackerel, scrapple, pepper sauce, and lemon wafers.

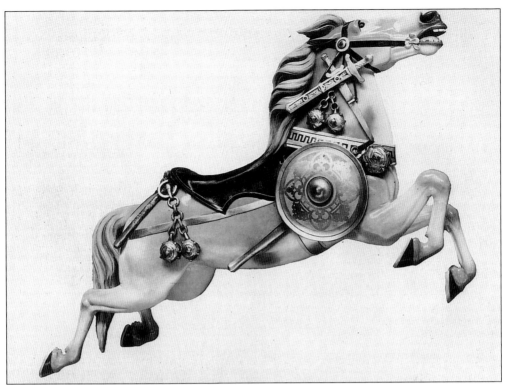

This carousel horse, a War Chariot Jumper, was produced in the Philadelphia Toboggan Company's workshop on East Duval Street. Master carvers such as Leo Zoller, Daniel and Alfred Muller, Frank Carretta, and John Zalar created these marvels. PTC carousels can be seen at Hershey Park and DisneyWorld. For the first time since 1932, the company is making a new carousel, which is for the Please Touch Museum in Philadelphia. (Courtesy of Philadelphia Toboggan Coasters Inc.)

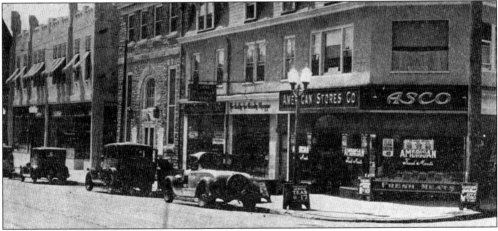

Mount Airy had a flourishing business district in the 1920s, including stores such as these on Germantown Avenue at Nippon Street. The market (American Stores Co.) is next to the Tally Ho Candy Shoppe, which remains today. Beyond that is the former Mount Airy National Bank and Trust, built by Samuel Harting, which is now offices. Next is Tourison building, which now houses a liquor store and day-care center.

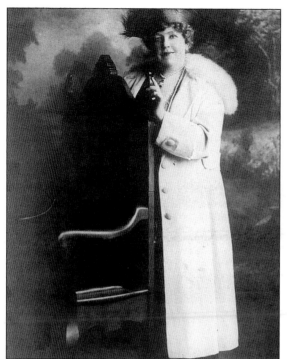

Charlotte Drake Cardeza was the daughter of a skilled immigrant textile worker who became a textile-mill owner. She lived lavishly and traveled frequently from her home, Montebello, a large estate on East Washington Lane. In 1912, she booked passage on the *Titanic* with her son, Thomas; her maid, Annie Ward of Chestnut Hill; and Thomas's valet, Louis Lesneur. All four survived the sinking of the *Titanic*. Charlotte Cardeza filed a claim of $177,352 for the loss of her jewelry and furs, but received little compensation. (Courtesy of Carol Kane.)

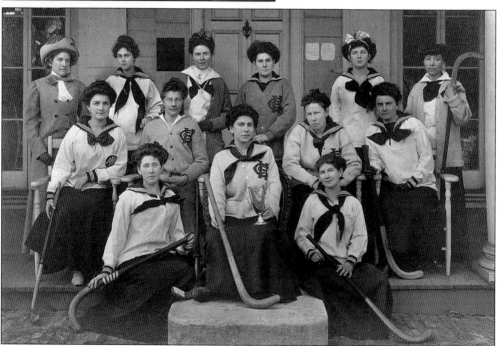

Hockey was brought from England to the United States in 1901. At first, women wore long skirts but soon switched to shorter ones that were all of 6 inches from the ground. In 1904, Carrie Wagner rounded up her friends in Germantown and taught them to play; teams and tournaments soon developed. The first captain was Violet Mange, pictured here with her team in 1908.

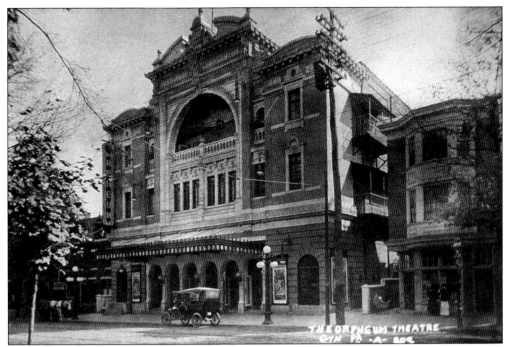

In May 1912, the Orpheum Theatre was built at 42 West Chelten Avenue. A marvel of brick and terra cotta outside and red plush inside, and with a Kimball pipe organ, it seated over 1,700 people. It began as a vaudeville theater, then in 1915 began to show movies as well. Other neighborhood theaters in the 1920s were the Germantown Theater and the Colonial Theater. The Orpheum was demolished in 1967. (Courtesy of Robert M. Skaler collection).

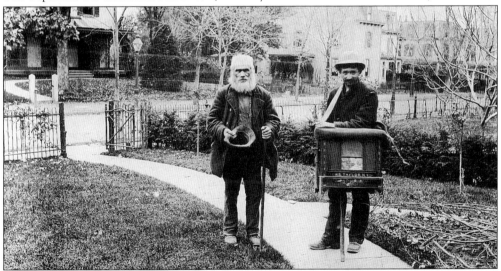

A hurdy-gurdy man and friend are seen on Walnut Lane in the 1920s. Other street entertainment at this time included organ grinders and small German bands. There were many street vendors, including a soup vendor calling "Pepp'ry Pot, nice and hot!", a man who bought soap fat, one who sold fresh horseradish, and one who called "Ice cream—hokey-pokey ice cream!" There were scissors grinders, oyster sellers, ragmen, and medicine men who sold the Elixir of Youth for $1 a bottle.

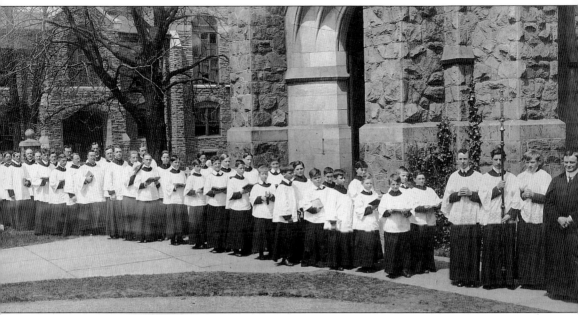

This photograph was taken during the choir festival of St. Luke's Choir of Men and Boys in 1915. The Reverend Samuel Upjohn was rector of the church from 1882 to 1923.

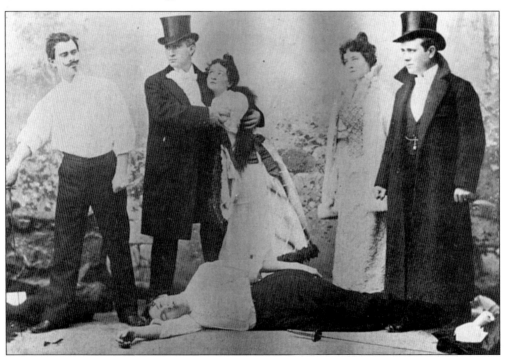

The talented Skelly brothers were the moving spirits of the Dramatic Club of the Enterprise Catholic Young Men's Association of St. Vincent de Paul parish. The Enterprise was a literary and debating club that flourished from 1871 for some decades. Both Mary Kennevan (stage name Mary Carr), center, and Mae E. Cody (stage name Maud Gilbert), right, seen here in *The Banker's Daughter* in 1893, went on to success in Hollywood.

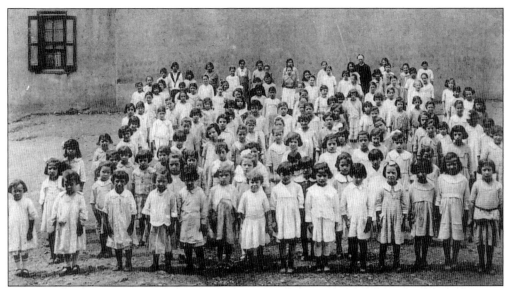

The increase in Italian Catholic immigrants to Germantown led to new churches and schools. The Holy Rosary Italian School opened *c.* 1913 at 334 East Haines Street with a few students, and an annex had to be built the following year to accommodate the 400 students seeking admission. The new building was dedicated with a parade and "scores of dwellings in the immediate neighborhood were decorated with American and Italian flags." In lower Germantown, St. Michael of the Saints Church was started in 1924 for Italians, while Irish Catholics attended St. Francis of Assisi Church on West Logan Street.

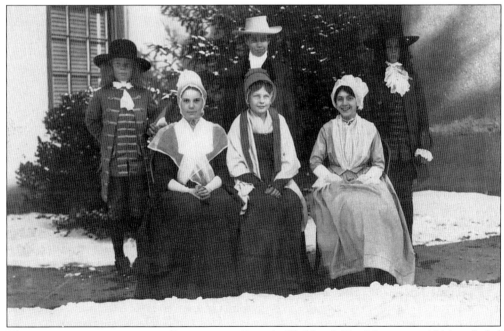

These young participants in a Germantown Friends Children's Tea Meeting in 1914 included Helen Dickey Potts, Annabella Bonnyman Wood, Mary Louise White, Gordon W. Strawbridge, Marriott C. Morris Jr., and John S. Wright, all in traditional Quaker dress.

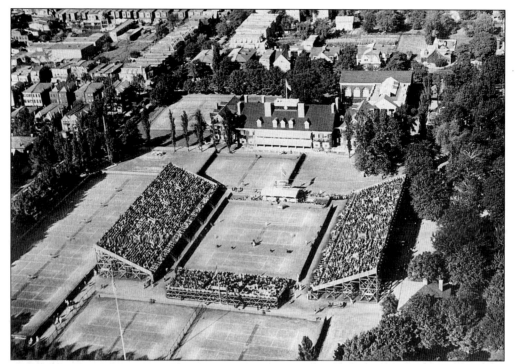

William T. "Big Bill" Tilden was born at Overleigh, 5015 McKean Avenue. One of the greatest tennis players ever, he won seven U.S. singles titles and ten Grand Slam singles titles in the 1920s, revolutionizing tennis with his powerful serve-and-volley game. The Germantown Cricket Club, seen here in 1921 during a tennis tournament, was the site of many of his triumphs. His reputation suffered in the 1940s when he was imprisoned in California on a morals conviction. (Courtesy of Print and Picture Collection, the Free Library of Philadelphia.)

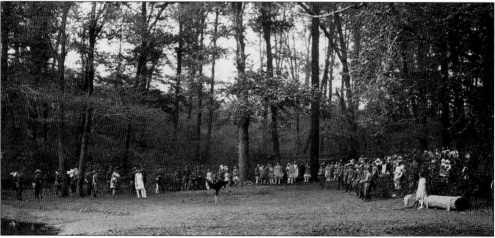

In 1921, students at the C.W. Henry School in Mount Airy, under the leadership of principal Caroline T. Moffett, established Philadelphia's first bird sanctuary in Carpenter's Woods. To raise awareness of conservation, students performed an annual Bird Masque in the woods. In the Bird Masque, a girl is saddened when a cardinal is shot by hunters. But the Spirit of Education persuades the hunters to throw down their guns.

116

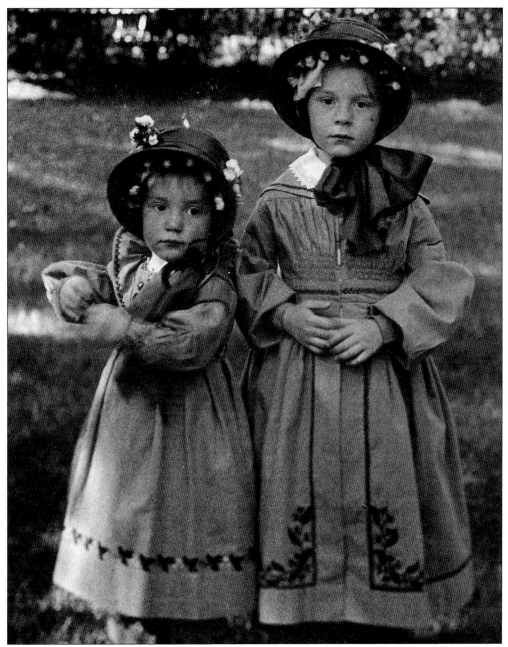

These two costumed girls are at a 1912 fete at the Germantown Cricket Club (formerly the Manheim Club) to benefit Germantown Hospital. The site was set up as "Old Germantown," with a Mystics' cave, the Indian Queen tavern, Enos Springer and the Tollgate, the old market at Market Square, shopkeepers, Mennonites, Quakers, and Native Americans ("under the leadership of Mrs. Owen Wister"). Also included was a miniature train representing the first trip made by the PG&N Railroad (including a stop at Stackhouse's for a glass of soda water "at the end of the grandstand" before the return trip), and assorted "characters," including Fiddling Ben, Crazy Nora, and chimney sweeps.

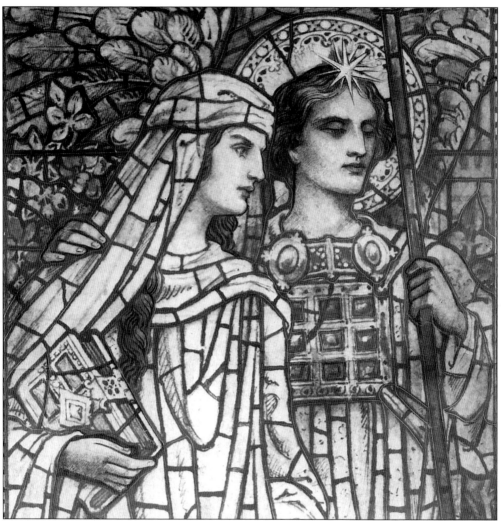

This 1914 stained-glass window depicting Christ Receiving the Soul is in Calvary Episcopal Church on Pulaski Avenue below Manheim Street. It comes from the Willet Stained Glass Studios, founded in 1898 by William Willet. Willet's son, Henry, took over the business and lived for a time in the Woodward family's icehouse at Springfield Avenue and Lincoln Drive. This family-owned business has now been in Chestnut Hill for 40 years. There are many fine stained-glass windows in local churches by Tiffany, D'Ascenzo, and others. (Courtesy of Willet Stained Glass Studios.)

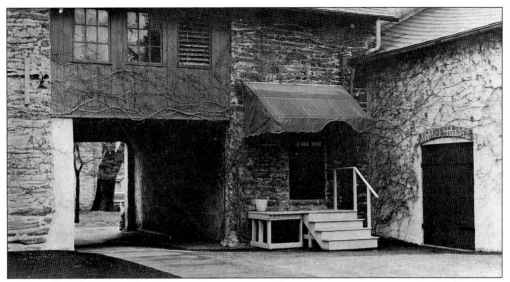

The active Stagecrafters theater group began in 1929 at 8130 Germantown Avenue in Chestnut Hill. Its first home was a one-story stone smithy from colonial times, set back 100 feet from the street. In 1936, the group rented a three-story house behind the smithy, and the two buildings were linked together.

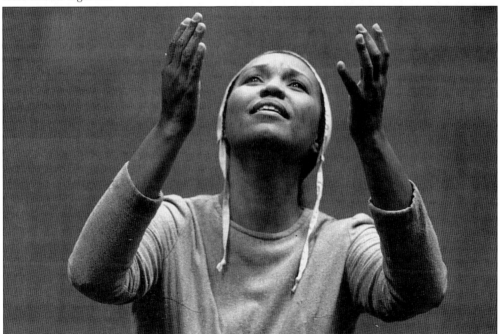

A complex of buildings at 4821 Germantown Avenue, formerly the Mehl House, has been home to the Germantown Theatre Guild since 1932. The Minehart family made the carriage house into a theater. They also offered touring shows such as *Sojourner Truth* (shown here with actress Cecily Patterson in 1997) to inner city schools, prisons, libraries, and senior citizen centers. The Theatre Guild was an early racially integrated company and for ten years presented free children's theater. Its artistic director, Katharine Minehart, was inducted into the Germantown Hall of Fame in 1997. (Courtesy of Germantown Theatre Guild.)

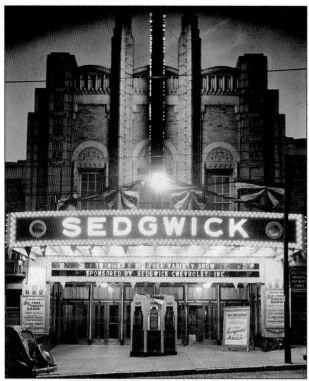

Mount Airy's business district was anchored until the mid-1960s by its art deco movie palace, the Sedgwick, built in 1928 at 7137 Germantown Avenue. Each show featured a movie, an organ concert, and a singer. In 1996, the Sedgwick Cultural Center formed to build community through the arts for both adults and children. It uses the lobby areas of the movie theater, but the theater itself awaits renovation. (Courtesy of Sedgwick Cultural Center.)

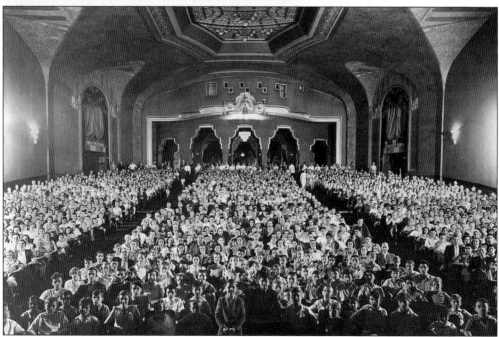

Designed by William H. Lee, the theater seated over 1,600 people and featured a cloister-vaulted ceiling. Both of these photographs are from a 1936 free movie variety show sponsored by Sedgwick Chevrolet, which was across the street. The Moller pipe organ is now at the Keswick Theater in Glenside, Pennsylvania. (Courtesy of Sedgwick Cultural Center.)

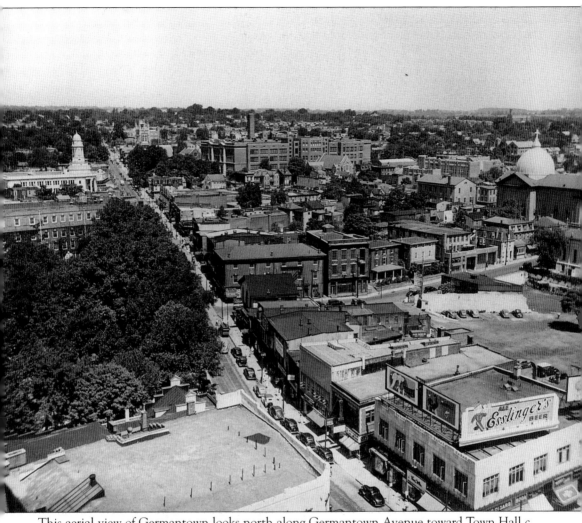

This aerial view of Germantown looks north along Germantown Avenue toward Town Hall c. 1936. Germantown High School and First United Methodist Church of Germantown can be seen top center. On the right is the dome of St. Vincent de Paul Catholic Church. The wooded area on the left is Vernon Park with the Founders statue visible through the trees. Above that is the YWCA.

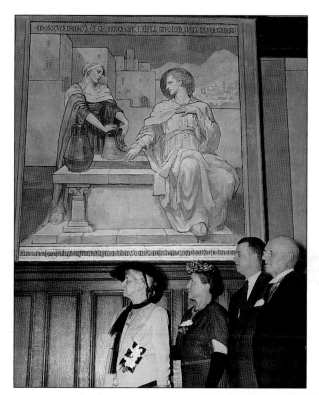

Violet Oakley was asked for a painting by the First Presbyterian Church in Germantown. She was so impressed by the room offered to her that she painted murals on all four walls, choosing as her subject great women of the Bible. She completed the commission in 1949. Oakley, seen here, left, at the dedication, was a noted muralist, stained glass artist, and illustrator. She lived and had her studio on St. George's Road in Mount Airy. Oakley is noted for the huge murals she painted for the Pennsylvania State Capitol building. (Courtesy of First Presbyterian Church in Germantown.)

George Allen's store opened in 1927 at Chelten Avenue and Greene Street as a new shopping area for Germantown. Typical merchandise included dresses, coats, hosiery, gloves, hats, umbrellas, wool and silk blankets, pitchers and vases, toiletries, and handbags. There was a separate department for men's clothing. Allen's was a fixture in the community and was the sponsor of a Santa and Christmas parade for the neighborhood, seen here c. 1960.

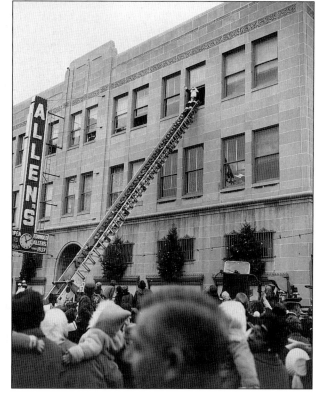

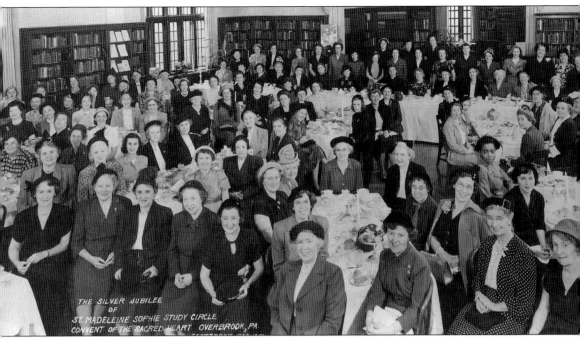

These women are gathered to celebrate the silver jubilee of the study circle of St. Madeleine Sophie Church in 1950.

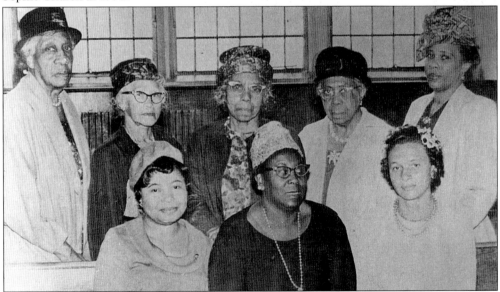

Faith Presbyterian Church was formed *c.* 1903 as the Tioga Mission and met in members' homes and elsewhere, including 304 West Coulter Street and the Wissahickon School Club. In 1914, a lot was purchased at 5331–5 Pulaski Avenue and the church's name was changed to Faith Presbyterian. An early member was Olivia Yancey Taylor, a respected teacher with connections to many local civic organizations. This photograph shows the board of directors of the Women's Organization at the 1964 golden anniversary celebration of the Church. In 1965, the Church merged with the Second Presbyterian Church to become the Germantown Community United Presbyterian Church at Greene and Tulpehocken Streets.

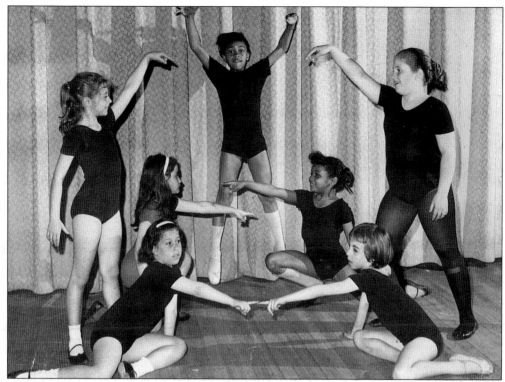

Allens Lane Art Center was started in 1953 as a way to bring people of all ages and backgrounds together through the arts. The following year, a summer day camp was opened. Mount Airy was becoming an integrated community and the camp was racially integrated—perhaps the first to be so in Philadelphia. Seen here in 1961 is a dance class taught by Jerry Packman. (Courtesy of Shirley Melvin.)

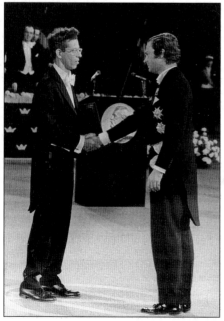

Howard Temin won the 1975 Nobel Prize for physiology and medicine. He grew up in Mount Airy on Hortter Street, graduated from Henry School, Central High School, and Swarthmore College, and taught at the University of Wisconsin-Madison. He was a cancer researcher who campaigned against smoking. A nonsmoker himself, he died of lung cancer at the age of 59. He is seen here receiving his prize in Sweden.

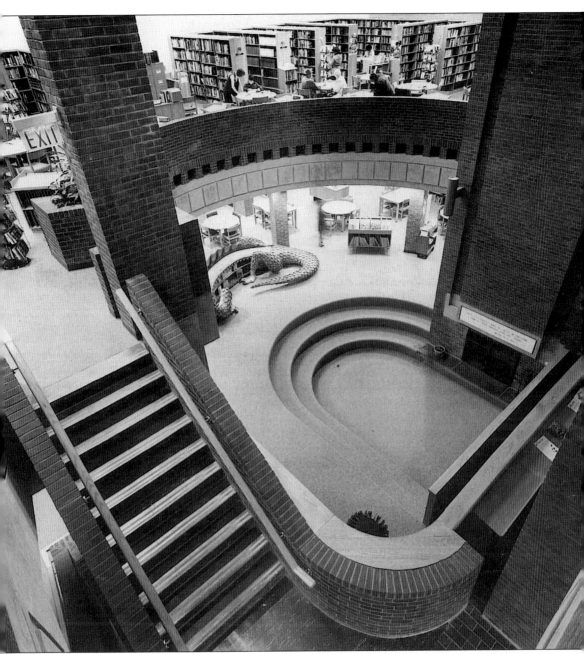

The Northwest Regional Library was built at the southeast corner of Greene Street and Chelten Avenue in 1978, in part due to the efforts of Councilman Joseph E. Coleman. It is on the site of the old Germantown Independent Gazette building. The library was supported from the beginning by an active Friends of the Library group. Seen in the children's area is a wooden dragon, named Regional Ricky by a patron, which offers a backdrop for storytelling and music. The dragon, which had been losing its scales, has since been restored and moved to a special platform. (Courtesy of Johnson/Smith Architects.)

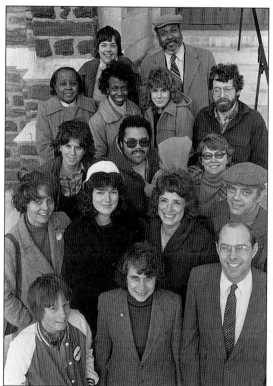

The Mount Airy Learning Tree was organized for the purpose of "learning from your neighbors." This photograph shows the organizing committee on the steps of the Krauth Memorial Library of the Lutheran Theological Seminary. From its 1981 semester of 16 classes, it has grown to over 100. Offerings reflect a wide range of neighborhood interests such as Chair Caning, African Dance with live drumming, Spanish, Dog Obedience, Belly Dance, and What To Do With Tofu. (Photograph by David Greenberg, courtesy of Mount Airy Learning Tree.)

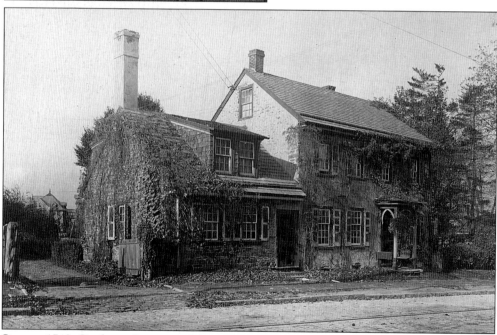

Since c. 1748, Cresheim Cottage in Mount Airy has been home to butchers, weavers, stocking knitters, hatters, furriers, powdermakers, printers, victuallers, a sheriff, a judge, and nurserymen. American troops fighting in the Battle of Germantown retreated past its front door. In an example of adaptive reuse, it was completely renovated in 1996 and is a successful restaurant.

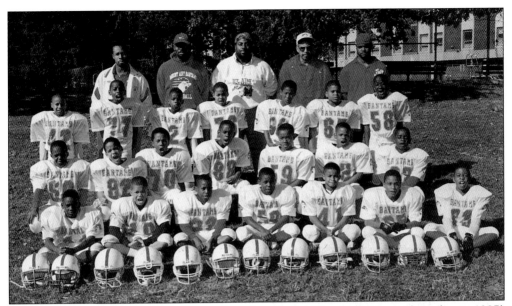

The Mount Airy Bantams football team (seen here is the 65-pound team and coaches in 1997) has members from Mount Airy, Germantown, Chestnut Hill, and elsewhere. They play at the Mount Airy playground on Sedgwick Street, formerly part of the Lovett estate. The city of Philadelphia acquired the property after WWII. (Courtesy of Eugene Stackhouse.)

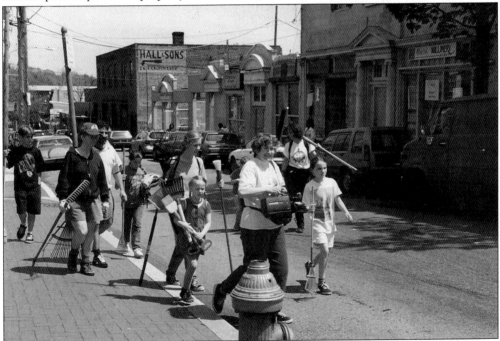

Thousands came out to spruce up Germantown Avenue on April 27, 1997 during the Presidents' Summit on Volunteerism. From North Philadelphia through Germantown, and from Mount Airy to Chestnut Hill, volunteers planted flowers, picked up trash, and painted murals. These volunteers on Church Lane are leaving the Germantown Historical Society on the way to their assignment.

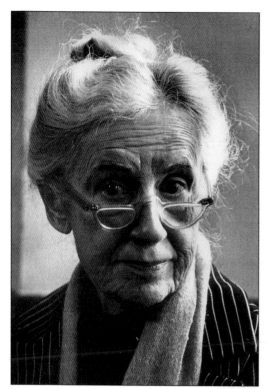

Margaret E. (Maggie) Kuhn (1905–1995) spent her life fighting for social justice. After facing mandatory retirement from her job, she and a group of women founded the Gray Panthers in 1970 to advocate for the elderly and to foster intergenerational relationships. She also started the National Shared Housing Program to encourage young and old to live together. She lived in such housing in Germantown for many years. She was inducted posthumously into the Germantown Hall of Fame.

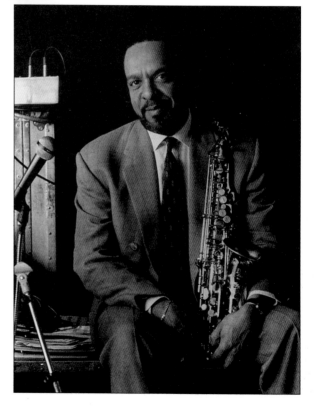

Grover Washington Jr., who died in December 1999, was another inductee into the Germantown Hall of Fame and a longtime enthusiastic resident of Mount Airy. A gifted saxophonist who was known for his unique ability to fuse pop, soul, and jazz, he won a Grammy for "Winelight" in 1980. He received numerous other awards both for his music and for his work in the community.